Copyright © 2016 Nick Amis
All rights reserved.

Disclaimer and Terms of Use: No information contained in this book should be considered as physical, health related, financial, tax, or legal advice. Your reliance upon information and content obtained by you at or through this publication is solely at your own risk. The author assumes no liability or responsibility for damage or injury to you, other persons, or property arising from any use of any product, information, idea, or instruction contained in the content provided to you through this book.

About this book

Have you ever wondered where all of the dogs come from for TV commercials and films? Are they professional, working dogs or just someone's pet who spends most of their time lounging round the house? Is there such a thing as a 'celebrity dog'? And can you make a living as an owner of a doggy superstar?

This book explains how to get your beloved pet onto the big screen, along with everything you will need to know to prepare. You'll never forget the first time you see you beloved pet on the TV or cinema screen. It's a truly magical experience for family and friends, one that neither you or they will stop talking about for years to come!

Testimonials

"As I read about the life of an acting dog and what is involved on film day, I found myself constantly thinking of little Hector. How nervous his owner must have been but so proud! I remember first seeing him on TV and was so shocked that I shouted, "That's Hector! He's a patient!! He's on the TV!!!" I just couldn't believe it. This book is well organised and packed with great information, such as how owners can care for the health of their famous pooch by checking them regularly at home. My customers get so excited just to see their pets' photo appear on our TV slideshow in reception; they are just going to love learning about how to hit the big time. Who knows, it may start a new wave of famous dogs from Higham Ferrers and put our little town on the map!"

Charly Middleton, Hector Longbody's vet

"A great read for all who dream of stardom for their beloved dog, great advice and guidance on how to develop your dogs skills ready for the limelight. Particularly love the training information giving detailed steps on how to achieve strong basic behaviours."

Annette Leslie, K9 Performance

About the Authors

NICK AMIS

Nick Amis is a writer and author but is also the owner of Hector Longbody - a black and tan miniature dachshund. Hector began his acting career with a series of commercials for a well known insurance company, with the campaign being run nationally during the Rugby World Cup and Six Nations Rugby tournaments. This high profile campaign catapulted him from relative obscurity to dog superstar, but also had the effect of dramatically increasing the popularity of the breed. Nick took the opportunity to write about his experience of the world of film and advertising to produce this hugely popular guide.

SANDRA STRONG

Sandra Strong is a qualified Veterinary Nurse, Dog Trainer and Animal Behaviourist. She also has a background in Theatre Costume Design, Stage Makeup and Wigs. After attending Wimbledon School of Art she earned a degree in Fine Art. She was an active member of The National Youth Theatre for many years, and later joined the Dolphin Company working with noted actors such as Vanessa Redgrave, Nyree Dawn Porter and Windsor Davis. In 2002 Sandra founded Dogs on Camera allowing these diverse careers to come together under one umbrella. Her dogs have appeared in Marie Claire Magazine , French Cosmopolitan and Bafta-winning docu-drama, "Brighton Bomb". Then came the first feature film, Rupert Everett's remake of St Trinians, featuring Dolly, the Norfolk Terrier whose performance as Mr Darcy afforded him The Fido's Award (Doggy Oscars). After that, assignments progressed at a steady rate until she received a call from a director wishing to produce a piece of work sponsored by Marmite for the Queen's Jubilee. Sandra had three days to find and train the dog. It was shown on large screens along The Mall during the

Jubilee Celebrations and the production company promised Sandra that if she succeeded in making this advert a success she would always be in work! The jobs have been flooding in ever since. Gratifyingly, she was informed by one of the Royal Correspondents that the Queen found the advert very amusing! Sandra has never looked back since and her dogs regularly appear on TV and film. You can watch a selection of her work on the Dogs on Camera website www.dogsoncamera.com.

Sandra also owns a company called Perfect Dog, London's premier dog training school. Sandra has developed her own unique style of dog training classes that allows owners to quickly and easily access the support they need. She has her own Film School for dogs, which prepares owners and their pets to work in front of the camera.

Contents

About this book 2

Testimonials 2

About the Authors 3

Introduction 6

Famous Dogs 9

What Makes a Good Celebrity Dog? 14

Step 1: Tip Top Condition 22

Step 2: How to Train Your Dog For The Limelight 34

Step 3: Creating a Resumé 83

Step 4: Finding an Agent 91

Step 5: Doing The Business 95

Step 6: Auditioning 102

Step 7: Preparing For The Shoot 105

Step 8: Lights, Camera, Action! 111

Step 9: After The Shoot 131

Step 10: Getting Your Next Piece of Work 134

Introduction

It was a Saturday morning and it was market day in Thrapston, England. Our family were all out dressed in our thick winter coats and Hector the Miniature Dachshund was along to make sure everyone and everything was in order. He likes to think he is the boss of everything. It doesn't matter how big it is or how scary it looks, in true Dachshund fashion if it looks like it needs barking at then that's what it will get. Hector landed his first major role on a TV commercial for Vitality Health Insurance. That year, Vitality were one of the main sponsors for the Rugby World Cup and Hector was the main character of the whole campaign. As we walked along the high street, we met an elderly lady who was out to shop for her weekly groceries. In usual dog-lover style, she bent down to say hello to Hector and stroke his silky smooth black coat. He is rather exceptionally cute and so small you could scoop him up and pop him in your pocket. She stood up and said, "He's adorable. He's just like the one on the TV." We looked at one another and smiled, "Well actually... he is the one from the TV!" My wife pulled her phone from her pocket and proceeded to show her pictures from the day of filming with the stars. As she did so, the elderly lady began to cry tears of joy. She was so thrilled to meet our little dog. "I can't believe it", she exclaimed. It was a good ten minutes before we were able to get away and continue our shopping. She even gave us her phone number and asked us to get in touch if we learned of any dachshund pups for sale.

This is just one example of the many wonderful experiences we have had introducing Hector the celebrity dachshund to his adoring fans. We never grow tired of people wanting to say hello to him, ask about his work or comment on how adorable he is.

It's amazing when you start to look at how often dogs appear on TV or in film. Just begin to count how many times you see a dog during commercials or during a TV show. I can guarantee that you will soon lose count because they are involved in just about everything. Celebrity dogs are big business because even the hardest of men can be turned into soft-hearted fools when they see an adorable animal doing something funny or cute.

Hector rehearsing with cell phone in paw!
We love this photo of Hector answering calls from his agent, posting his Twitter and Facebook updates and checking his email

Just where do all these dogs come from? Are they professional, working dogs or just someone's pet who spends the rest of their time lounging round the house waiting for their next star appearance? Can you make a living as an owner of a dog-star? How does one go about turning their dog into a celebrity?

- What kind of special training will my dog need?
- Does my dog need to have super abilities?
- Are some dogs more likely to be famous than others?
- Does my dog have what it takes?
- What are they looking for when choosing a dog?

- Will it take a lot of my time?
- Will I have to invest a lot of money?
- Where do I start?
- Will I make money from it?
- Is there such a thing as a celebrity dog?

This book explains everything you need to know about how to have a chance to see your beloved family pet on the big screen, along with everything you will need to know to prepare. There are no guarantees of success but you'll certainly have a lot of fun along the way. Even if they don't make it big in film or TV there is always the prospect of Internet fame. Some animals have more followers than even the biggest of human celebrities. After all, isn't the Internet powered by dogs and cats? Every second piece of news or entertainment is either a dog or cat doing something particularly amazing, stupid or just downright hilarious. We love our pets and they will never be far away from our hearts. They make our lives more complete in so many ways.

You'll never forget the first time you see you beloved pet on the big screen. It's a truly great experience for family and friends.

So, sit back and relax and listen to how you might achieve stardom, fame and celebrity for your pooch.

Famous Dogs

Celebrity nowadays is more popular than ever, it's almost as if it can be a career choice for youngsters when they leave school. "What would you most like to be when you grow up, little Jennie?" "I want to be famous." Amazingly you can become famous for just about anything, thanks to the power of the Internet. People who have developed a large online following are now crossing over into the mainstream and appearing on TV and in films.

Now you may not be familiar with Crusoe the Celebrity Dachshund with his 809,848 Facebook page Likes and 58,076 YouTube Channel subscribers, but you may have heard of Lassie, Hooch, Beethoven, Big Red, Old Yeller, Marley, Toto, Milo, Einstein, Benji, Eddie, Rin Tin Tin, Comet. These A-Lister dogs world have, at times, dominated with their numerous prime time viewing appearances; some even out-earning their human counterparts.

Toto in The Wizard of Oz

Toto, played by Terry, was paid $125 a week which was more than many of the human actors. She went on to appear in 13 different films

In many cases the dog has not just been a co-star in a major movie but they *are* the star. There have even been whole movies featuring only dogs. In the 1920s there were as many as 80 acting dogs in Hollywood. From 1954 to 1973, there were almost 600 episodes of Lassie produced. More recently we've enjoyed seeing Benji in no less than seven films. Are dogs taking over? Are they going to put us all out of work? Well, maybe that's going a little too far. Certainly they seem to be here to stay and continue to be a vital element in many films, TV shows, advertising campaigns, music videos, books, magazines, online videos, social media channels, and the list goes on.

Marley the Labrador

A very successful tear-jerker starring Owen Wilson and Jennifer Aniston

There have also been memorable dog performances in very successful TV commercials. Sammy, the Jack Russell, appears in a popular series of commercials for GoCompare, an insurance comparison website. In one particular advert, Sammy is dressed in a costume that makes him look as if he is two dogs carrying a box! Another very popular series of commercials were Walls

Sausages where a dog sang a 'thank you' song to various people. This works very well with audiences; after all, who doesn't love a talking dog?!

Sammy the Jack Russell as Piano Dog

Sammy also appears as Double-Dog in the popular TV Commercials for GoCompare

DOGGIE OSCARS

Believe it or not but there are even Doggie Oscars. That's right. Film Awards for dogs.

The **Palm Dog Award** is an alternative award presented during the Cannes Film Festival. Started in 2001 by Toby Rose, it is awarded to the best canine performance. The award consists of a leather dog collar with the words "PALM DOG" written in gold lettering. The name "Palm Dog" is a play on words of the Palme d'Or, the festival's highest accolade. The awards were inspired by his own fox terrier and muse Mutley, now sadly departed, who had appeared on TV, starred in fashion magazines, and met a considerable number of stars – Steven Spielberg, Charlotte Rampling, Chloë Sevigny.

The **Golden Collar Awards** started in 2012 and are organised by the website Dog News Daily. The first Awards rolled out the red carpet for the dogs on the 13 February 2012 at the Hyatt Regency Century Plaza in Los Angeles. A notable winner was Uggie the Jack Russell Terrier for his performance in The Artist.

The **Fido Awards** are international awards for canine movie stars. Founder Toby Rose wanted to create a British awards ceremony for pooches, and in 2007 the Fido awards were launched at the British Film Festival.

Dolly the Norfolk Terrier with dog handler Sandra Strong

Dolly's exceptional performance won her two Fido
Awards for 'St. Trinians'

When the production company for St Trinians contacted the agency Dogs on Camera they were desperate. "We need your help! We have tried all the other agencies and they have said what we are asking is impossible." They wanted a dog to hump an actor's leg on command. Preferably a terrier. It took Dolly just 15 minutes to learn the basis of this action and a video was quickly produced. She was called to audition two weeks later having perfected the action, which was put on verbal command "Go for it Dolls!". Dolly was cast as Mr Darcy and appeared alongside Rupert Everett and Talulah Riley in the 2007 remake of the classic St. Trinians film. She won Best International Comedy Dog Actor and Best International Dog Actor for her performance.

What Makes a Good Celebrity Dog?

Working in the 'Film World' is like working in a microcosm of the real world. The level of training needed in this world is far greater than any regular obedience course that your dog might have been on. If you want your dog to appear in front of the camera, you must pay a great deal of attention to detail. You are going to need to train your dog without suppressing their personality; they need to appear confident and natural. They are going to need to be able to work with actors and work alone.

The answer to the question "What makes a good celebrity dog?" is flexibility and an ability to quickly understand what the trainer is requiring them to do. They will need to be reasonably extrovert and have a great deal of charisma in order to win the hearts of many. It will also greatly depend on you and the amount of time and dedication you can give to training.

Movies & TV Series

Dogs in movies are often required to perform a wide range of tasks and tricks such as putting their paws over their eyes, lying down and shutting their eyes on command, and standing up on their back legs and so on. To be selected for a film role your dog will need to be able to demonstrate that they can perform a wide range of tricks, as well as be capable of learning new tricks in double-quick time.

The types of dogs used in movies range greatly. It depends on the story line and what that demands the dog to do. Some breeds are easier to train than others and that may mean picking one dog over another. However, if the breed is key to the story, a dog of that particular breed will have to be found to perform the tasks required. Lola, the black Pug from the Molly Moon movie, had to rip the sleeve off the villain's jacket, walk around with a chocolate biscuit in her mouth, open cupboards and pull objects out from under a bed! These are the actions of a Labrador and a German Shepherd, not a Pug!

Ability is not always the overriding factor. Appearance is also very important when choosing a dog for a role. The casting director may have some idea of what they are looking for, but they need to see the dog before they are sure that they have the right one. You will often be asked to attend an audition.

But there is a more practical matter regarding the choice of dogs for films: It is necessary to have more than one acting dog for the role because dogs cannot work for lengthy periods of time. It is not uncommon to have two, three or even four dogs that play the role of one dog in a film. The original Andrex Advert used 30 Labrador puppies! For that reason all the dogs must look alike so that the audience will never know that it's not the same dog. You may find your dog being picked primarily because it looks exactly like another dog, even if your dog cannot do all the required tricks. One dog may be used for the complicated tricks and another for the simpler tasks.

Some breeds and colours are more popular for starring roles. For a family movie, which most dog movies are, a friendly or cute-looking dog is more likely to get the starring role. The most popular colours are tan, brown, tan-white-black with black and darker coloured dogs being less likely to land a starring role. That said, all breeds, sizes and colours of dog are used within movies in some way or other.

The other main consideration for working on a movie is the amount of time it takes. Your dog may be required to be on set for several weeks, depending on their role within the movie. Most pet owners would not want to be away from their dog for extended periods of even if there was a qualified dog handler taking care of them. This means that you would probably need to have the time available to be working with your dog.

Music Videos

Even pop videos feature dogs. Normally not dancing but certainly involved if the video involves telling a story. And just because it's a music video doesn't mean that they will not be acting whilst the music is playing. The sound is added afterwards.

Most of the same rules apply as for a film albeit production times are much shorter.

Kylie Minogue cuddles Chidley the black Labrador
Lucky Chidley was picked to star in Kylie's Christmas
Single video even though he has a black coat

TV Commercials

Roles for TV commercials are more straightforward than for movies. They are obviously a lot quicker to produce, with many productions being filmed in one day. Due to the nature of commercials, the scripts are quite short and therefore they are a lot more accessible to the average pet owner. That said, you'd be surprised how much they can pack into a 30-second slot of TV. Even just 30 seconds of TV can take an entire day of filming and I mean a 6am start and midnight finish!

Typically dogs only need to be able to do what is laid out in the story board, which in some cases may be to sit in one spot and do nothing else. With very little to no training, your pet could be the star of a commercial. I have seen dogs with no training at all picked because they just looked like another dog that was previously used. However, you should always be prepared for a last-minute request to do something that is not in the script.

Ralph the Poodle and friend star in this commercial for Philips
The dogs had to wear some great costumes during filming

When it comes to selecting the right dog for a commercial, it is not uncommon for the client (the company the advert is for) to be involved. After all, the dog will be representing their brand and product. For this reason, your dog's appearance and movement are even more important. Most clients are very fussy when it comes to who is representing them and are unlikely to pick any breed that could have a negative connotation.

Commercial Photo-shoots

It is quite often the case that photo shoots will be done in conjunction with filming. The main cast is taken to one side after filming for interviews and photos. Depending on the dogs role in the production, they may also be required to be photographed. Dogs and their handlers are increasingly being interviewed these days as it is popular to run a feature on the making of the commercial on You Tube, thereby maximising the reach of a particular campaign.

Some assignments do not involve any film work and are just photo shoots. This is more often the case for print e.g. books and magazines.

Buddy the Dachshund on set for Frontline
Buddy appears in a magazine advertising campaign for Frontline

Shoots can be in a studio or on location and may require static poses or action shots. Just because it's photography doesn't mean that your dog won't be required to perform tricks. They may want your dog in a particular pose and to hold that for a duration whilst the photographs are taken. They may be required to jump, bark or roll over.

This type of work can be the most difficult for a dog to perform as they may need to hold a *Stay* position for a long time, perhaps as long as 10 to 15 minutes. They may also need to follow commands during the *Stay* such as looking up and down, flicking their ears and so on, all without getting up. This would need to be performed off-lead and with endless distractions such as make-up artists doing touch-ups, perfecting the models, set designers adjusting the stage, lighting changes, cameras not working, you get the idea.

The Internet Celebrity

In all of the above cases you are dependent on your dog being chosen for greatness. When it comes to the Internet you can, with very little investment, broadcast your dog to the world. There are around 1 billion people with a Facebook account and several hundred million people on Twitter, Instagram, LinkedIn, Google+ to name but a few of the social media sites. That means there is a huge potential audience that may be interested in your dog.

Boo, the world's cutest dog!

Boo's owner is a Facebook employee who created a page for the Pomeranian back in 2010. His online popularity soared when Ke$ha tweeted a message saying she had a new boyfriend and linked to Boo's FB profile. The page quickly hit five million followers and the dog was offered a publishing deal – that book has now been printed in 11 different languages, and Boo is the 'spokesdog' for Virgin America Airlines. He generates approximately $1 million in revenue every year.

There are few qualifications or rules about what makes an internet celebrity. What's important is that your dog is there to entertain and delight. It's totally up to you how to present your dog to the world and what is going to keep people interested.

Let's Get Started

Step 1: Tip Top Condition

Just like their human counterparts, dogs need to be fit and healthy to work, no matter how old they are. Doggie actors come in all shapes, sizes, and ages. It is never too late for your dog to become a star. You CAN teach an old dog new tricks.

Dogs are our responsibility to look after as they can't do it themselves. You must make sure your dog is in tip-top condition if they are to stand any chance of achieving celebrity. It is important you take your dog to the vet for regular check-ups to ensure they are in tip-top condition for their age. Before your dog can appear in a production, they will need a Health Certificate from their vet to show they are fit and able to perform the tasks required. As well as visiting the vet, there are some checks that you can do at home between visits.

GENERAL CONDITION

We cannot stress how important it is for regular vet check-ups. It is also important you check your dog's general condition when you perform your dog's daily groom. Keep a check on your dog's adult weight (this is the weight achieved when the animal is around 18 months and should be noted by your vet). Learn to touch and feel your dog all over for loss of body mass, swellings, hard lumps and infestation of parasites. This is especially important if your dog has long fur.

Make sure your dog maintains the correct weight for its breed and size throughout life. Always pop your dog on the scales if you visit the vet. Changes in weight are not always visible in long, densely-haired breeds. So regular grooming and handling are essential.

There should be a vet on duty when you are attending a shoot. If you have any concerns regarding your pet's health or welfare, please feel free to discuss any issues with them.

Here's how you can check your dog's weight:

- Make sure your dog is standing up (you may need to tempt them with a small treat)
- Run your hands over your dog and get a good feel of their body, paying particular attention to ribs.
- You should be able to feel the ribs but they shouldn't be visible or sticking out at all.
- Check your dog's spine. You should be able to feel it but not see it.
- Check your dog's waist (behind the rib area). You should be able to make out where the waist comes in.
- Move down to your dog's back end. It should feel firm without indentations.
- Make sure you weigh your dog twice a year at the Veterinary Surgery

Iraida the Afghan Hound looking gorgeously groomed

NEEDS TO BE CLEAN

Grooming is not just about keeping your dog looking good or maintaining your dog's cleanliness. Good grooming is also about maintaining both your dog's physical health as well as appearance. To achieve this, you need to use the correct tools for the job.

Before you use any grooming equipment on your dog, let them sniff the implement first. Next, slide the comb or brush once through their fur. Now that it has the dog's scent on it let them sniff it again. In this way they will be accepting of the comb or brush. This small exercise often stops dogs turning and trying to bite the grooming implements.

Combing and brushing your dog regularly prevents your dog's coat from forming matts. Slicker brushes are good for removing dead hair, dirt and dandruff and finishing your dog's coat. It is important to use a comb if your dog has long hair. Grooming brings out the natural oils in the dog's fur giving a healthy sheen. It is also a useful way to get your dog used to being checked over for health issues.

Regular grooming will ensure that your star-in-waiting is looking their absolute best for auditions and when on set.

NEED TO BE HEALTHY

It is really important to ensure that you dog is fit and healthy. Wanting the absolute best for your dog starts by keeping them as healthy and happy as possible. No one is going to want to use an unhealthy dog for a production. To keep your four-legged friend in tip-top shape, give them a regular once-over using our check-list at the end of this chapter.

FLEA TREATMENT

Flea treatment should be given every few months. Use a good quality veterinary flea treatment as cheaper ones can be less effective. If your dog already has an infestation, you will need to treat your house as well as the dog. Regular vacuuming and washing of the dog's bedding will also help. Remember to keep a record of when they had their treatment and put a reminder in your diary for the next one.

WORMING

You should be giving your dog worming treatment every three months when working in the film industry. A worm infestation cannot only cause health problems to your dog but can, in some cases, spread to humans and has been known to cause blindness. Again, make sure to use a quality product or simply purchase them from your vet.

VACCINATION

Make sure you protect your pets and keep them safe by keeping up-to-date with their vaccinations. By vaccinating your vet each year, you will protect your dog from potentially fatal diseases.

New-born pups are protected from infections by their mother's maternal antibodies, which are passed by the placenta to the unborn pup and by the colostrum (the first milk), but only if the bitch has been regularly vaccinated. However, this protection only lasts a few weeks and they will need to start a vaccination program at eight weeks of age. It is not advisable to bring a young pup into contact with older dogs, because even if the dog in question has been vaccinated, they can still carry disease. They should not be brought into a studio environment before they have completed their initial course of vaccines.

Failure to properly vaccinate your dog not only endangers their life but makes them a potential risk to other dogs and to people. Infections such as Leptospirosis can be spread to humans by coming into contact via the urine of an infected dog. Such infections can cause kidney failure and even death.

MICROCHIPPING

Protecting your pet is not just about their health; protecting them from being lost or stolen is increasingly important. Microchipping is largely recognised as one of the most effective ways to protect your dog's identity. Implanting a chip is safe and relatively inexpensive to get done. Speak to your local vet and they will be able to help you.

NEUTERING

There are varying opinions as to whether it is advisable to get your dog neutered. Some advisors recommend neutering if you are not planning to breed from your dog. For bitches, it does have the advantage of preventing unwanted pregnancies, and it can also protect their health and unwanted attention from male dogs. Certainly you do not want to be working your dog if they are in season. If you want your Bitch to have regular film work with a season twice a year could be a real disadvantage. A bitch in season can be a messy business, it can also cause your bitch to become moody and broody, resulting in a phantom pregnancy, which could mean she is unable to act for several months. In the case of un-neutered male dogs, marking on set could be a potential hazard due to expensive electrical equipment. Do make sure to seek the advice of your local vet.

House Training

Now you may not think that going outside to the loo is a major priority, especially for smaller dogs shy of cold and wet weather, but for a dog working on set, this is very important. Before considering working your dog you must ensure that they are properly house trained. No one is going to be very happy if your beloved pooch tinkles over the star of the show or leaves a present for someone to stand in. There are also potential health and safety risks, since there is a lot of electrical equipment around on set.

5 Steps to Successful House Training

1. For short periods when you can't supervise your dog, put them into their pen, indoor kennel or crate. This helps because they have an inherited tendency to keep their rest area clean. This is also a good policy when your dog is not working on set. Keeping a crate nearby to the set, allows your dog to rest in a safe place between takes and know you are nearby. This also has the advantage of making it easier for you to organise toileting times around that famous word: ACTION!

2. Take your dog to the area you want them to use for toileting when they wake up, are excited or have finished eating. This will help them develop an association with the environment and surface. Praise and treat them when they perform in the correct place. If you take Alpha treats with your dogs, make the association with doing their business in the correct place that much faster. Give them the treat just as they are about to finish. When they are anticipating the treat, you can put this activity on command - very useful when you have a film sequence requiring them to do it.

3. For puppies, give them further opportunities to go at least every two hours when awake. Learn to spot when they are restless, sniffing the floor or circling, squatting or crouching. Lift them and take them to the toileting area. It is also advisable to house train puppies in conjunction with crate training. Puppies should have at least three good sleeps a day. This gives you three clear opportunities during the day when you can be sure your pup will want to pee. Like us, when they wake up they generally have a full

bladder and will want to relieve themselves. Carry them out of their crate so they cannot get excited and piddle on route to the garden door, then place them in the garden where you would like them to go. Praise and treating will make the association to go outside more quickly and puppies are often 85% house trained in just three weeks! Although do expect accidents up to six months. If your puppy does have an accident in doors clean up with an agent that has a biological content to break down the proteins in the urine (the pup will smell the protein content and relieve itself again in the same place). DO NOT reprimand your pup or rub their nose in their urine of faeces as the lining of your pup's nose is delicate and sensitive. Doing so could cause a great deal of damage and they could also inhale this toxic material into their lungs.

4. At first, puppies may not be able to make it through the night, so plan to stay up late and get up early. You may need to get up in the night as well.

5. Using pads and newspaper is for your convenience when cleaning up afterwards but your puppy may learn the wrong place to go. Instead put the pads or paper down where you want them to go, gradually reducing the amount once the correct location is being used. When your pup relieves themselves on these articles do not praise them, just clear it up. Some breeds do not mind positive or negative attention, so if you tell them off they may interpret the attention as a reward. Your pup needs to understand that they get no attention when they perform inside. When they do go outside, treat them and give attention in abundance so they make the association of going outside more readily.

LASTLY

You should consult a vet if you have any doubts about the health of your dog. Online tools are not a substitute for a professional qualified veterinarian.

WHAT YOU NEED TO DO

To give your dog a health check they need to be happy for you to touch them all over their body. If at any point they are not happy with being checked over, then stop and try another time. Take a note of which bit they did not like being touched as this could be a sign of pain. Don't try and treat anything you find without first consulting a veterinarian. After their check-up make sure you give them plenty of praise and treats. This is usually taught in Puppy Class when the dog is around 10 weeks old. It is important your pup feels comfortable and calm, and gets used to gentle restraint before you start checking them all over. Performing Ear Slides (stroking your puppy's ears) and T-Touches (gentle body work) along their back releases endorphins and makes your puppy sleepy and therefore more receptive to being handled. Always be gentle and talk to your puppy in a quiet, happy voice when you start your handling exercises.

Check	✔ / ✘
EARS The best way to check the ears is to lift the ear flap and spread the flap over the head of the dog so you can see into the ear cavity. It should look a pale pinky shell colour. There should be no redness, no discharge and no smell. If you observe any of these conditions, especially if you have noticed scratching or head shaking, seek veterinary attention straight away and do not start feeling around your dog's ears as they could be very painful.	

Check	✔ / ✘
MOUTH Remember this area can be treacherous, so make sure you get it right! Puppies have very sharp needle teeth, and older dogs have much larger teeth and stronger jaws. Start by very gently stroking your dog around their lips. When they are happy with this, lift up the lip with your middle finger and massage the gums (we perform this exercise on young pups so they are receptive to teeth cleaning). With pups, make sure the teeth are erupting correctly. With older dogs, check levels of tartar and that there are no cracked or broken teeth. Take this opportunity to open your dog's mouth to check for soft tissue injuries and inflammation of the throat and gums. An easy way to open a dog's mouth is to squeeze very gently behind the canine teeth (the long pointy ones), as this causes the bottom jaw to become slack and the mouth is easily opened. If you have any cause for concern, consult your veterinary surgeon.	
EYES The easiest way to look at your dog's eyes is to position yourself behind your dog so they are facing away from you. Place one hand under the jaw and the other hand on the top of the head. Perform little strokes on top of their head to keep them calm. Place the thumb from your top hand above your dog's left eye then place your thumb from your bottom hand under your dog's left eye, gently open the eye. The inner eyelids should be a pale pink, they should not look red or have any discharge. Repeat for the right eye. If you are concerned, consult your vet.	

Check	✔ / ✘
NOSE The nose on a healthy dog should feel moist and cool. There should be no purulent discharge. This, along with excess sneezing and distress, could indicate a foreign body. Sneezing, snorting, and coughing could be a sign of a Kennel Cough. Your dog should not have a dry cracked or bleeding nose. If any of the above occur, consult your vet.	
BODY Get used to feeling your dog all over every day when you pet and groom them. If you do this, you will notice any lumps and bumps and note if they are changing in size. Any lump that is growing rapidly needs to be checked by a vet immediately. When you are combing and brushing your dog, check for excessive hair loss. Remember, twice a year your dog will moult; this is normal. Always check areas where matts occur such as under the armpits, around the groin area, behind the ears and under the tail. If you run the comb through these areas daily you will prevent the build up of dead fur. Check fur lodged in the brush and comb for flea dirt. Sometimes, it is difficult to distinguish these from specs of mud. If you are not sure, sprinkle some of this residue on a sheet of damp kitchen paper. If the specs of dirt turn red then your dog has gas visitors - fleas! Check for excessive scratching and nibbling or sucking, especially in the groin area; this can lead to bald patches and definitely needs to be checked by a vet.	

Check	✓ / ✗
FEET Dogs can have very sensitive ticklish feet and often do not like them touched (this should be tackled in puppy class). Start by gently stroking the top of the feet with your thumb, then place your middle finger in front of the large pad in the middle of the foot and spread out the toes. Check for any matts, mud or grit. Also check if the skin between the feet appears moist and sticky. If your dog is giving this area particular attention, you will need veterinary advice. Check the claws including dew claws (these can be found along the inner side of the dog's foot). Some dogs have rear dew claws. These claws do not wear down during exercise and will need clipping regularly. Check all claws for hooked ends as these will need removing. When clipping claws do not clip beyond the quick.	
BOTTOM In order to inspect your dog's bottom it will need to feel comfortable with you lifting its tail. Begin with gentle strokes and T-Touches around the base of the tail, then gently lift the tail. If you have a long-haired dog make sure there is no faecal residue on the feathers beneath the tail. Wash and remove faeces from this area as it could attract flies and they could lay their eggs around this area, causing considerable damage. Loose motions could be a sign that your dog is unwell. Check your dog's bottom for worms, and worm eggs. If your dog is passing blood in their faeces, consult your vet. Either side of your dog's bottom are the anal glands. Sometimes these can become full and not empty, which can cause your dog to rub its bottom along the floor. This means a trip to the vet to get them emptied. Your vet will advise you as to why this is happening.	

Other signs that your dog might be unwell are: Being lethargic or restless, not eating or eating less, excessive drinking, keeping to themselves, not wanting to be fussed, growling when touched or out of the ordinary behaviour.

Step 2: How to Train Your Dog For The Limelight

Many people aspire to be famous, to be adored by millions, to have a life of luxury and not to want for anything. What they may not realise is that most of those people have worked very hard to get where they are and continue to do so. Making it big can take a lot of time and commitment. It's not all sitting by the pool sipping margaritas. No, there have been many sacrifices made along the way to master their skills, develop their presentation, go to auditions, work long days, as so on. Yes, there is a fair amount of luck involved but the chance of success is greatly improved when combined with hard work.

Damon the Alaska Malamute

We love this picture of Damon with his wig and wink.
I think he likes this look too!

This can also be true for dog actors. Apart from the fact that it's you that will be doing most of the hard work - they'll just be having fun playing great games and receiving treats, praise and attention! You'll need to help your dog master the necessary skills and behaviours so that they stand the best chance of beating the opposition.

In this chapter we going to look at some of the basic skills your dog will need, as well as some more advanced tricks that will stand you in good stead when asked to do the impossible on set.

SOCIALISATION

One of the most important aspects of any dog's training is socialisation and habituation. Socialisation involves your dog being comfortable and relaxed with a wide variety of different people, including children, people using disability aides, people with crash helmets, men with beards, hats, and much more. The aim being for your dog not to be afraid or disturbed when coming into contact with new, strange looking people. They should get on well with other dogs and behave normally when in new places.

Puppies socialising

Often vets and trainers will run pup socialisation sessions where you can take your dog along to meet and play with other dogs

Habituation involves your dog being confident in their immediate surroundings. They should not feel afraid if they hear a loud bang (studios are noisy places), worried by unfamiliar objects, such as black plastic sacks or household appliances. Remember, they may be helping advertise them after all!

Being social is really important when working, because they are going to come into contact with a lot of people, some strange and unusual, other dogs and new places. It's going to be difficult if they are barking and snarling at others when they are supposed to be following the script. To become a well-rounded dog star, your pup needs to have had an extensive socialisation period, as well as some very basic training procedures put in place, before they can go to the next level.

Typically, socialisation needs to be completed between eight and 12 weeks old. Any older and it becomes increasingly difficult to accustom the dog to new things. However, this can be overcome with patience and training, so don't despair if you feel your dog has missed out on this time period. Aim to introduce your dog to as many different types of people, animals and places as you can, but under controlled conditions. Please do not buy a buggy. (One lady actually did this.) She went through the list of of habituation targets by placing her young puppy in a buggy and leaving it in front of each one for ten minutes. This included pneumatic drills, dust carts, etc. The poor pup ended up traumatised!

ADULT DOGS

Dogs are at their most receptive when they are between three and 12 weeks old. So the earlier you socialise them the better. After 12 weeks it can be very difficult to get a dog to accept anything new or unfamiliar.

Unfortunately, it is not always possible to complete socialisation within this time. You may have re-homed a dog or the vet may have recommended keeping them away from other dogs and places. Here are some tips on how to socialise an adult dog:

Walk your dog daily introducing them to other people and dogs. Walking them and letting them run will use up some of that pent-up energy.

Remain calm even if they are barking or growling at others and don't tell them off. Move them away from the situation. Reward them when their negative behaviour changes. Carry some medium value treats with you to give to willing strangers who may like to help in the socialisation of your dog. It is essential for dogs to have an association with new experiences followed by a positive outcome.

If you are struggling to correct unwanted behaviour, there are lots of trainers who can help you.

What You Need To Do

Use the following checklist to socialise and habituate your dog. Please be sensible and do not position your dog near anything that gives off very loud noises; remember their hearing is very sensitive. The best way to introduce your dog to many of these experiences is to sit with them outside your local coffee shop. Tick off each item as you complete it.

People	✔	Places & Surfaces	✔	Sounds	✔
Men		Other People's Homes		Vacuum cleaner	
Women		Parks		Birds	
Boys		Parties		Barking	
Girls		Crowds		TV	
Babies		Sporting event		Music	
People with glasses		Shopping malls		Sirens	
People on crutches		Bridges		Bells	
People with walking sticks		Woods & Forests		Door knock	
People with beards		Fields		Cars passing	
People with hats		Out in the rain		Whistle	
People in wheel chairs		Subways		Meow	
People walking strangely		Tunnels		Lawn mower	
Other dogs		Trains & Buses		Children playing	
Cats		In cars and near traffic		Hammering	
Other animals		Tiled floor		Drilling	
People running		Wooden floor		Hair dryer	

People on bikes	Carpeted floor	Chainsaw
People on skate boards	Laminated floor	Remote-controlled cars
People on hover boards	Grass	Sliding doors
Thin People	Gravel	Fireworks
Heavy People	Tarmac	Thunder
People in costumes	Snow	Gunshot
People in big coats	Leaves	Cheering
People of all races	Earth	Shouting
People dancing	Rug	Crying
People playing music	Puddles	Laughing

Weird Things	✔	Situations	✔	Travel	✔
Brooms		On the leash		Cars	
Balloons		Having eyes cleaned		Escalators	
Kids toys		Collar hold		Stairs	
Plastic bags		Having ears cleaned		Planes	
The wind		Wearing a harness			
Fast movement		Clippers		**Other Animals**	✔
Flags		Being held		Puppies	
Umbrellas		Having mouth opened		Big dogs	
Baby strollers		Muzzle		Small dogs	
Big plastic objects		Grooming		Other breeds	
Shiny objects		Being carried		Shaggy dogs	
Big balls		Cutting nails		Farm animals	
Frisbees		Loom overhead		Rabbits	

Mirrors	Being washed	Birds
Shopping Trolleys	Being body handled	Mice & rodents
Tents	Being bandaged	
Thrown things	On a table	
Flashlights	Teeth cleaning	
Bean bags	Vets	
Running water	Being gently restrained	
Crates & boxes	Isolation	

As well as socialising your pup yourself you should also try and involve strangers as much as possible. For example, ask a friend to groom them, put a muzzle on, open their mouth, etc. Make sure your friends take time to win your dog's confidence before embarking on these procedures. Using treats is often a way to a dog's heart! The dog's compliance in these actions should make them more comfortable around strangers.

Positive Training vs Correction

A consequence of any behaviour can be pleasant or unpleasant. The rationale of the human mind dictates punishments should follow unwanted behaviours, just as rewards follow good behaviours. Research shows that although punishment decreases the frequency of unwanted behaviour, it usually results in producing another. The results of punishment as a training method are difficult to predict and to control. In addition, the dog cannot always understand which particular behaviour it is being punishment for, since it almost always comes after the event and is rarely clearly connected with a specific behaviour. In the dog's mind, the punishment is a random, meaningless event. It is, therefore, less effective than positive reinforcement when it comes to training a dog.

Trainers and owners feel that their relationship with their dog is stronger and more rewarding when they focus on the positive rather than the negative. The main difference is the attitude and enthusiasm of the dog who is working to earn rewards, rather than to avoid punishment. However, it is a good idea to give young animals boundaries, otherwise their normal puppy behaviour can easily get out of control, for example with nipping. The best way to do this is to use your voice - a high happy voice when your puppy is being good and a deep growly voice when the unwanted behaviour is in full swing.

Clicker Training

Clicker Training is the 21st century method of training your dog. It is a fun, effective way of teaching dogs everything from simple obedience to complex tricks. A clicker is a small plastic box with a hinged piece of metal sheet inside. When you press the button, the metal sheet makes a "click" sound.

The process is very simple. Decide what behaviour to teach and when the dog does something that looks like that behaviour, mark the action with a click. The way it works is the dog becomes tuned into the sound, knowing every time they hear the click they are doing something right and will be rewarded.

It is important to be quick when clicking. You need to be able to click at the exact moment your dog is doing what is being asked of them. Not before the action and not after. For example, if training them to sit, click the exact moment their bottom touches the floor.

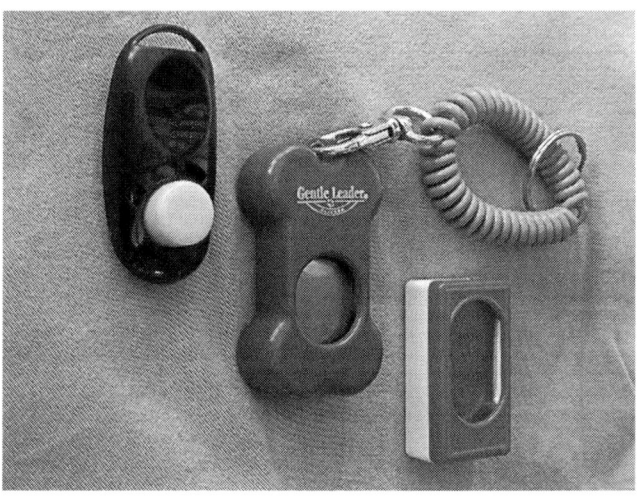

Various types of clickers

Clickers allow you to mark precisely the action your dog performs, for which they are being rewarded

The essential difference between clicker training and other reward-based training is that the animal is told exactly which behaviour earned the reward. This is communicated with a distinct and unique sound, a click, which occurs at the same time as the desired behaviour. The reward then follows.

In the early stages of clicker training, it will be necessary to reinforce the positive association with the click, by giving your dog a small treat.

Tuning to the sound of the clicker

The first thing you will need to do is tune your dog to respond to the clicker. We do this by associating a reward with each click.

1. Sit at a table with a bowl of treats.

2. Put the lead on your dog; their position at this stage is not important.

3. Hold the clicker in one hand and put it behind your back. **Click** and reward your dog with a **Treat**. It is important to give the treat quickly.

4. Repeat this action about 20 times. For every **Click**, you must give a **Treat**.

5. Now let your dog off the lead.

6. Wait until they are not seeking your attention and occupied, but not engrossed in a game.

7. **Click** the clicker.

8. If they look up and come for a treat then they are tuned into the clicker.

9. If they do not respond, then repeat the above exercise.

Once they consistently respond to the click, you are ready to start teaching your dog anything you want. Once your dog starts to understand the exercise you are teaching, you can wean them off the clicker and eventually the treats.

How to Teach using a Clicker

There are seven stages to training.

1. **Click** to mark the wanted behaviour and **Treat**.

2. Repeat at least 20 times until your dog is consistently performing the behaviour.

3. Introduce a cue for the behaviour e.g. a command or visual movement with the hand.

4. Give the cue, **Click** to mark the behaviour and **Treat**. Repeat at least 20 times.
5. Gradually eliminate the **Click** when your dog is performing on cue.
6. Gradually eliminate the **Treat**.
7. Repeat training at a different location e.g. outside or in a strange place.

If at any stage your dog is not progressing when you try to move to the next step, simply go back a step.

Skateboarding is easier than you think!

Renowned dog trainer, Sandra Strong, teaches dogs to skateboard using a clicker, on their first lesson

It is important that you resist the temptation to say "Good dog", or stroke your dog's head when using treats to reward them. Give the treat to them immediately after clicking for the desired behaviour. At this stage, the treat alone is their reward.

Do not repeat the exercises in one session; spread them out during the day and when you start your next session, start on the previous stage but move to the next stage quickly. Although you may not get tired or bored, your dog will, or they may fill up on treats and no longer want to be rewarded. Try to keep each training session to no longer than 30 minutes. Lots of short training sessions are far more effective than one long session.

WHAT YOU NEED TO DO

Learning to clicker train

1. Purchase yourself a clicker.

2. Choose a type of treat for your dog (see later chapter on treats).

3. Tune your dog to the clicker.

4. Set aside regular times during the day to have training sessions with your dog.

Remember, it can take time and you need to be patient. Give your dog time to think things through. You will be surprised just how bright many dogs are, they can often work out what you want them to do. With the right treats, dogs will try just about anything to get that reward!

And last of all, make it fun and give them plenty of praise when they do it right.

TREATS

Treats are a valuable and essential part of any dog training program. After all, your dog is working so they should receive payment!

Treats should be something that your dog enjoys, that will have them giving you their full attention. If you find that they are easily distracted during training even though they are hungry, then try a different kind of treat.

There are lots of things to choose from that are good for dogs such as chicken, ham, cheese, crispy bacon or sausage. Find out what really motivates your dog. For our miniature Dachshund, Hector, it's ham. He will do absolutely anything for a piece of ham.

Treats should be chopped up into small pieces, about half the size of your smallest finger nail. Treats should be small for two reasons. The first is we don't want them to be spending a lot of time eating during training sessions; a couple of chews and it should be gone. The second reason is that we don't want them filling their tummies because once they are full they are going to quickly lose interest in training. However, it is a good idea to keep a few large treats to grab your dog's attention should they get bored.

It is sometimes useful to place treats on a saucer or plate, so they are easily accessible.

Homemade Alpha Treats

Alpha treats are good quality, highly palatable pieces of food. They should arrive in your dog's mouth as small bursts of flavour. Alpha Treats are useful when doing particular training exercises such as Recall, as the high motivational value of the treat is more likely to achieve the desired result.

Examples of Alpha Treats are: liver, sausage, beef, chicken, frankfurters, bacon, lamb.

Ham is a popular treat with dogs
A handful of finely chopped ham should be sufficient for
full hour of training for any sized dog.

Low Grade Treats

Low Grade Treats also have a place in dog training. A low grade treat is one that is less tasty and appealing than an Alpha Treat. If you have a breed that is well known for having a keen appetite, you may find Alpha Treats cause the dog to become over enthusiastic, making it difficult to calm them in order to move on to the next exercise. It is is useful to grade your treats depending on what you are teaching your dog.

Oven baked dog biscuits
Dried treats still need breaking up into small pieces.

Low Grade Treats are better used for Leave training, as your dog is less likely to lose self-control and make a grab for the treat. When using Low Grade Treats for training exercises you must also break them up into very small pieces.

Examples of Low Grade Treats are: oven-baked dog biscuits, toast, vegetables.

Commercial Treats

There are many commercial Alpha Treats to be found in pet shops and in supermarkets. Soft, meaty snacks are very useful. They are usually produced in flat strips, which easily crumble into small pieces. They also fit the grooves of interactive toys.

BASIC TRAINING

We are now going to look at some of the basic things that you can train your dog to do. You may have already mastered some of these, which is great. There is no need to use the clicker if your dog is already consistently responding to the commands or cue you are giving. Should their response not be consistent, than re-train them using the clicker method.

These basic behaviours will stand you in good stead not only in everyday life with your dog but when in front of the camera with 50 people stood round, waiting for the call of 'Action' from the director.

George the Bulldog demonstrates his excellent Down

Although he's looking half asleep, he keeps a watchful eye on his handler, waiting for the command to be given to get up

THE WATCH

An often forgotten part of training, but an essential one when it comes to instructing your dog, is The *Watch*. It is difficult to teach your dog anything unless they pay attention to you. This is essential for a young pup, because if they don't look up at you, they could quite easily lose sight of you when out and about, become very frightened and bolt. This exercise is useful on many levels and is more beneficial than *Sit* or *Down* in the early stages of training.

Smiller, the Labrador carefully watches and waits

Smiller has appeared in TV commercials for Blue Cross
and a hilarious April Fools commercial involving
payment cards for dogs

1. Put your dog on a lead.

2. Place a plate of **Treats** on a high table out of reach of your dog.

3. Take a **Treat** and put it on your middle finger and cover it with your thumb.

4. Hold the treat under your dog's nose.

5. When they notice the **Treat** slowly move your hand round so they are facing you.

6. Introduce the cue "What's this?" and immediately give them the **Treat**.

7. Working quickly, take another treat and repeat the cue, gradually lifting your arm up higher.

8. Wait until they look at your hand and repeat the cue "What's this?" and **Treat**.

9. Keep the exercise going very fast until your hand is above your head. Your arm and hand should be in the position of asking a question in class.

10. How you need to add time by counting in seconds to measure your dog's attention.

11. Count to five seconds and **Treat**. Continue in multiples of five.

12. You can combine this with the *Stay* to get your dog to remain looking at your hand.

At no point should the dog be looking into your eyes. They should be looking at your hand.

SIT

The *Sit* is one of the easiest commands to teach your dog. When your dog is sitting on command, they are easier to manage until they learn more self-control. For example, when the doorbell rings, they are less likely to jump on visitors when obeying the *Sit* command.

Hector, the Miniature Dachshund demonstrates the sit

Not the easiest to tell if his bottom is on the floor since he hasn't very far to go from standing! Hector has appeared in a high-profile advertising campaign for World Rugby.

1. Get on your dog's level, either on the floor or in a chair next to them.
2. Hold a **Treat** close to their nose. Their head should follow the treat as you move your hand.
3. Slowly move your hand upwards.
4. As their head tilts up to follow your hand, their bottom should lower.
5. When the bottom hits the floor **Click** and **Treat**.
6. Repeat 20 times per training session.
7. Introduce the command *Sit* before moving your hand upwards.

8. Gradually eliminate the **Click**.

9. Gradually eliminate the **Treat**.

DOWN

This *Down* is slightly harder than a *Sit*. Give your dog time to figure out what they need to do to get the treat, and don't rush them. If necessary, hold the position and wait to see if they figure out what is being asked of them.

1. Place your dog into a *Sit*.

2. With a **Treat** held between your thumb and middle finger, place it in front of your dog's muzzle.

3. When they notice the **Treat,** move your hand towards the floor.

4. They should follow the hand that conceals the **Treat**.

5. As your dog's head follows your hand, slowly move your hand along the floor away from them.

Colin and Dudley, the Border Collies, do a tandem Down

Dudley has appeared in a three-minute film for The Fright Fest Season, called "What the dog saw", and also starred in "Britain's Favourite Dogs".

6. Their body should follow their head and stretch out into a down.

7. As soon as their tummy touches the floor, **Click** and **Treat**.

8. Release your dog from the *Down*.

9. Repeat 20 times per training session.

10. Introduce the command *Down* before moving your hand towards the floor.

11. Gradually eliminate the **Click**.

12. Gradually eliminate the **Treat**.

If your dog makes a grab for the treat in your hand or they try and sit up, take your hand away and reset to the start position. Never push them into a *Down*.

STAY

So what's the difference between *Stay* and *Wait* I hear you say? Aren't they just different words for the same thing. Well, no. The difference is that wait is given with the expectation of another command following, whereas stay is indefinite.

Hastings, the Dachshund demonstrates an advanced standing Stay

The stay is a very useful command on set when you want your dog to hold a particular position or to stay where they are. Hastings appeared in a TV commercial for Matterssons as a homage to Hank Marvin.

You would give a *Stay* when leaving your dog in one position without giving them any attention. A well executed *Stay* means that your dog is exactly where you left them when you return.

Stay is a calm exercise. When your dog hears the command, they should sit calmly and patiently waiting for your return.

1. Place your dog into a *Sit* in front of you.

2. Position your dog so they are quite close to you.

3. Leave your one foot in front of your dog and move the other foot back half a pace.

4. Return your foot. **Click** and **Treat**.

5. If your dog appears calm, repeat the command and take a whole step back.

6. Return to your dog. **Click** and **Treat**.

7. Gradually increase distance and wait time before returning.

8. Introduce the command *Stay*. You can also point to indicate *Stay*.

9. Gradually eliminate the **Click**.

10. Gradually eliminate the **Treat**.

It can take time to build up to a very long *Stay* without your dog coming to you. If you find that you dog cannot hold the *Stay,* then reduce the distance and time away and repeat.

RECALL

Your dog should return fast as the recall signal is now a neutral sound, which does not show any anger, frustration, or fear which they may detect in your voice. If you have been yelling their name and reprimanding them for not returning to you, their *Recall* could be getting worse, not better. They may have a bad association with *Recall*.

This sound is associated with an Alpha Treat and the promise of a game. For this training exercise you will need a squeaky toy small enough to keep in your pocket.

DX, the Labrador being recalled

The recall is a really great command to teach your dog, even if it's only for their own safety and your sanity. On set, it's a great way to get your dog to come in your direction to get the required action.

1. Place your dog in front of you.

2. Squeak the toy in your pocket.

3. When they pay attention to the squeak, **Treat** immediately. In this way, we are teaching them to associate the sound with receiving a **Treat**.

4. Keep the exercise going very fast to build up the association.

5. Now put everything away for 20 minutes.

6. Wait until your dog is elsewhere in the house or garden.

7. Now squeak the toy so they can hear.

8. If your dog comes to you, **Treat**. If they come very quickly, then give them three **Treats** one after the other.

9. When you can, sneak off without your dog seeing you and hide somewhere.

10. Squeak the toy so they can hear it. Hopefully they will start looking for you.

11. **Treat** when they arrive.

12. Introduce the command *Come*.

13. Gradually eliminate the squeak.

14. Call your dog in a high, happy voice.

Once they respond reliably, then you can play this game in the park and when out for walks. Don't let your dog get too far from you. Keep squeaking and **Treating** throughout the walk. Never give your dog the squeaky toy during training and only let them off the lead when it is safe to do so.

SPEAK

Teaching your dog to speak is remarkably simple. Especially for dogs that like to bark. It's getting them to be quiet afterwards that can be a challenge!

In this exercise, we will refrain from using the clicker.

Gibbs the Crossbreed talks the talk!
Gibbs starred in Britain's Favourite Dogs

1. Show your dog a large **Treat**; a whole sausage or a favourite toy is a good choice.

2. Tease your dog with this and pretend to walk away.

3. Reward any sound, even a squeak, with a small piece of the sausage, or by throwing the toy.

4. Repeat the process until the dog becomes more vocal.

5. Once the dog is barking, introduce the cue word *Speak*.

6. The next step is to introduce a signal, such as tapping your fingers and thumb together.

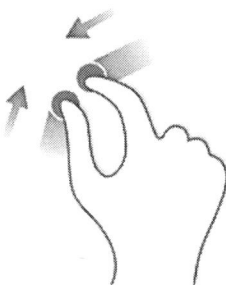

7. Hand signals are important when filming because if sound is running you will not be able to give verbal cues.

HEEL

Have you ever seen a dog owner being towed down the road by their dog? Or perhaps you are that dog owner, whose dog takes them for a walk rather than the other way round. Well, we're going to look at how to have your dog walking by your side without pulling.

We're going to look at two methods of training for this particular exercise.

Jake the Labrador walking to heel

Dogs often need to stand by the actor or walk to heel during filming, so this is a really important skill to learn. Jake demonstrates this perfectly with stick in mouth!

Using Target Training

1. Place your dog in a *Sit* on your left side.

2. Place the palm of your hand in front of your dog's nose. Their natural curiosity should make them nudge your hand. **Click** and **Treat**.

3. Move your hand slightly forward and take a step. **Click** and **Treat**. If you have a small dog you can use a Target Stick.

4. Increase your steps gradually and lengthen the times between the **Click** and **Treat**.

5. Add a cue word *Heel*.

6. Gradually eliminate the **Click** and **Treat**.

7. Once you can travel at least 10 steps, put the dog's lead on and continue.

8. This exercise should be practised around the home and garden, before being used along the road.

Using a Loose Lead

1. Place your dog in a *Sit* on your left side.

2. Clip on the dog's lead (a two-metre training lead is preferable).

3. Hold the lead in your right hand and adjust the length so it runs diagonally across your body, hitting your left thigh.

4. Take a step forward, if your dog comes with you and stays by your side **Click** and **Treat**.

5. If your dog pulls ahead, then stop, and turn round so your back is towards your dog (facing back to where you started). Call your dog to you by looking over your left shoulder. When they return, turn round clockwise so as to

bring your dog with you, until they are back in the original position on your left side. **Click** and **Treat**.

6. This time quickly take a step forward. **Click** and **Treat** as soon as your dog comes to your side. Do not give them the chance to pull ahead. They need to understand that if they want a **Treat** they need to stay by your side.

7. Repeat and continue to **Click** and **Treat** when they are by your side.

8. Gradually increase the distance between **Click** and **Treat**.

9. Add the cue word *Heel*.

10. Gradually eliminate **Click** and **Treat**.

Target Training

Target training is one of our favourite exercises and is quite simple to do. So what is target training? It's sounds like we're going to teach your dog archery! Not quite. Target training is getting your dog to focus their attention on an object and perform some action towards it. The most common actions are paw-touch and nose-touch.

Troy, the Jack Russell shows off his soccer skills!

Touching objects is another frequently used trick in films and commercials. Getting your dog to do this on cue is going to put them streets ahead when it comes to their auditions.

Target training with the paw

1. Place your dog into a *Sit* in front of you.

2. Place a high value **Treat** in your clenched fist.

3. Offer your fist to your dog at a level they can easily touch it with their paw.

4. As soon as they touch your hand with their paw, **Click** and open your hand so they can receive the **Treat**.

5. Once your dog is performing on a regular basis, use the cue word *Touch*.

6. Gradually eliminate **Click** and **Treat**.

Target Training with the nose

1. Place your dog into a *Sit* in front of you.

2. Hold the back of your hand at a short distance from your dog's nose.

3. Your dog's natural curiosity should make them nudge or sniff your hand. **Click** and **Treat** as soon as they nudge your hand with their nose.

4. Now begin to move your hand from side to side, so your dog has to get up to nose your hand. **Click** and **Treat** when they nudge.

5. Once the dog is doing this continuously, add the cue word *Nudge*.

6. Gradually eliminate **Click** and **Treat**.

HEAD DOWN

Dogs spend most of their time just lying around, sleeping, contemplating the meaning of life. It's what they are pretty good at. That is, until you come along and they just want to play. Getting them to do what comes naturally can be a bit of challenge, but that's what the producer is going to want - them acting naturally.

In this exercise, we're going to look at how to get your dog to put their head down and look like they are relaxing.

Barny the Chocolate Labrador with head on paw

After years of practising the art of slobbing out, he demonstrates the art of looking relaxed on cue. Notice how he continues to pay attention, waiting for his next command.

Head Down onto floor

1. Place your dog in a *Down*.

2. Using a **Treat**, lure your dog's head down to the floor between their paws. **Click** and **Treat** as soon as their head is down (leave the treat on the floor for them).

3. Lengthen the time before the **Click** in order increase the time your dog's head stays on the floor.

4. Once your dog anticipates your action of luring their head in-between their paws, give them the cue *Head Down*.

5. Gradually eliminate **Click** and **Treat**.

Head Down onto paw

1. Place your dog in a relaxed *Down*.

2. Using a **Treat**, lure move your dog's head so it is resting on their paw. **Click** and **Treat**.

3. Once your dog is anticipating the luring action, give them the cue *Head on paw*.

4. Gradually eliminate **Click** and **Treat**.

SLEEP

Training your dog to mimic their favourite pastime can be a tricky business. It will require a fair amount of patience on your part. It's best taught when your dog is naturally tired, perhaps after a long walk.

In order to complete this exercise successfully you will need to have mastered other skills in advance such as: *Down* and *Stay*. We're not going to use the clicker as this tends to put them in a state of alert and we want them as relaxed as possible.

Joey Spaniel taking a controlled snooze

A genuine sleep is quite tricky because it requires the dog to close their eyes on cue while anticipating a treat they cannot see!

1. Place your dog into a relaxed *Down*. You could do this in your dog's bed to start with as it may be easier.

2. Give your dog the command to *Stay*.

3. Sit down on a seat near to your dog and remain quiet.

4. If your dog starts to look sleepy and their eyes start to close, say very quietly, "*Close Your Eyes*" and **Treat**.

5. Quietly repeat the command *Stay* and return to your seat.

6. As soon as the eyes close, repeat the command *Close Your Eyes* and **Treat**.

7. Keep repeating.

8. Now, before your dog becomes sleepy again give the command and watch to see if they close them.

9. As soon as their eyes close, **Treat**.

10. Begin to hold off on giving the **Treat**, making your dog wait longer after closing their eyes.

11. You're almost there!

Well done if you manage to crack this one as it can be particularly tricky. There are no prizes for trying to teach this one while your dog is actually asleep!

ROLL OVER

Many dogs love to roll over on their backs. You may see them doing this with other dogs, to demonstrate that they are not a threat, or when playing with their toys. It can also be a very useful trick to perform while on-set.

Ruth the Welsh Corgi in 'dog heaven'.

Ruth had to lie on her back as petals rained down on her in a TV Commercial for Body Shop. It was part of an advertising campaign for Mother's Day involving the Queen!

1. Place your dog in a relaxed *Down* where there is plenty of space around them.

2. Make sure they are settled and comfortable.

3. Hold a **Treat** on their nose without letting them take it. Now lure their head around to their shoulder by moving the **Treat**. Their head should naturally follow your hand. **Click** and **Treat** when their head reaches their shoulder.

4. Repeat, but this time take the dog's nose a little further over the shoulder. **Click** and **Treat**.

5. This time, take the head as far as it will go and now the feet should follow and your dog should be on their back. **Click** and **Treat**. Note: Be careful not to drop the treat into their mouth when they are on their back, because it could fall down their throat and cause them to choke.

6. Now introduce the command *Roll Over*. You should be able to now perform the exercise without having a treat in your hand.

7. Once your dog is anticipating your lure directive, eliminate the **Click** and **Treat**.

THE TAKE

How often do you spend time looking round the house for something, only to find it has been taken by your four-legged friend? A missing slipper, the post, a set of keys - is there no end to the kleptomaniac habits of your dog. So what could be better than actually teaching them to take stuff on command?

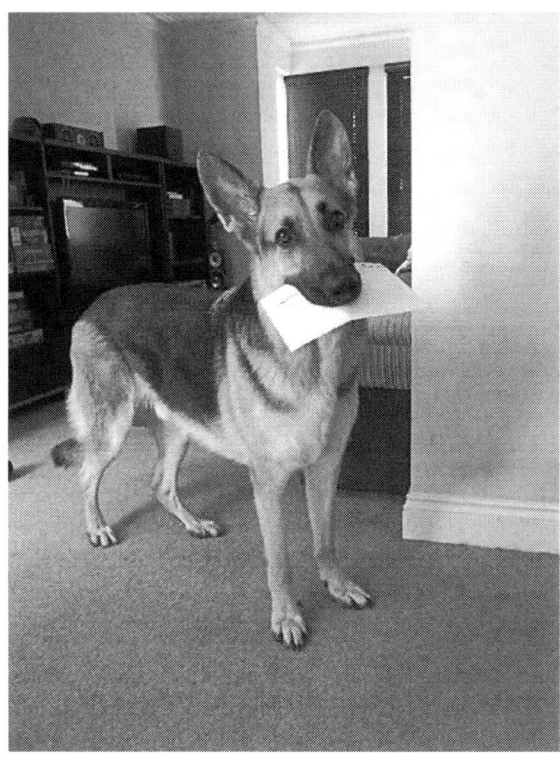

Awesome the Alsatian demonstrating The Take

Awesome, the talented German Shepherd, plays frisbee, pretends to be dead, carries a newspaper and plays with a boy in a TV commercial for lungworm awareness.

The Take (using play)

1. Select an object you would like your dog to *Take* and *Hold*. In the early stages of training, make sure this is something quite resilient. A rag toy is a good object choice. Try to use one your dog has not seen before.

2. Start by having a gentle game of tug.

3. Now let go of the toy and let the dog hold on to it.

4. Count to five and then swap the toy for a **Treat**.

5. Repeat several times, adding the cue word *Hold*.

6. Gradually increase the time in seconds your dog holds the toy.

7. Now decrease the game and encourage the dog to *Take* the toy themselves.

8. Eventually you should have them taking on command.

The Take (using Target Training)

1. In this method, we using Target Training. We do not use a clicker because you will find your dog opens their mouth too quickly to get the treat.

2. Show the dog an object you want them to hold.

3. When they nudge, **Treat**.

4. Let them nudge the object several times always giving a **Treat**.

5. Now withhold the **Treat**. Your dog will now typically nudge the object several times in frustration then, with any luck, they will mouthe the object. As soon as they do, **Treat**.

6. Let them do this a few times, then withhold the treat again until they take the object.

7. Now begin to wait for a few seconds while they are holding the object, before swapping for a **Treat**.

8. Add the cue *Hold*.

9. Repeat the exercise until your dog picks up the object themselves.

10. Now add the Cue word *Take*.

11. Gradually eliminate giving a **Treat**.

Costumes

Costumes are a vital part of any film, TV show or commercial, and this is often the case for the animals too. Your dog may need to be a particular character in a story and will need to wear a particular costume, such as a bandana, a hat or a suit!

It's important to stress how important it is to ensure your dog is comfortable in their costume and not keep it on longer than is necessary. Allow sufficient time for your dog to become familiar with it, and become accepting of wearing it.

If your dog is used to wearing coats when going out for a walk, then they usually do not mind dressing up in other outfits.

Sammy the Jack Russell in costume

Sammy looks absolutely fabulous in his 'Double Dog' outfit. This TV Commercial for GoCompare was a great success.

1. To introduce your dog to a new costume first let them sniff it, then give a **Treat**.

2. Repeat until they are happy to accept the costume.

3. Now start to dress them, giving a **Treat** at every stage.

The same principles can be applied with wigs, spectacles, shoes, etc.

WAVE

There is nothing quite as charming as seeing a dog mimicking a human action, such as waving. As if they were not adorable enough, now they have to be even more loveable by copying what we do.

Esme the French Bulldog demonstrates a Wave

Some dogs have a natural instinct and can sense what it is you want them to do. Esme is a very talented actor.

1. Place your dog in the *Sit* in front of you

2. Place a high value **Treat** in a clenched fist and offer your fist to your dog in range of their paw.

3. When your dog goes to touch your fist with their paw, withdraw your hand so your dog's paw is left waving. **Click** and **Treat**.

4. Keep repeating this exercise until the dog realises that this is a new action.

5. Now introduce the cue *Wave* and gradually reduce the **Click** and **Treat**.

Distance Work

It's one thing to train your dog to do what you want them to do on command, but it's something else getting them to do it when you're not nearby and saying nothing at all. For film work it is often the case that everyone will need to stay completely quiet during filming, and that includes you! Furthermore, they won't want you in frame with the actors. This means you'll need to give instructions to your dog from a distance and without saying anything. We call this *Distance Work*.

Hand Signals (*Sit*)

Hand signals need to be seen at a distance so your actions have to be large and exaggerated. The hand signal for *Sit* is a large scooping movement, with the elbow bent, bringing the palm of the hand over the shoulder.

1. Place your dog in a *Sit* in front of you but at a distance.

2. Entice your dog forward with a **Treat**.

3. As they approach, perform the hand signal for *Sit* and give the command for *Sit*.

4. Repeat this exercise six times, three with hand signal and voice, and three with just hand signal.

Dogs learn this very quickly! Now, every time you ask your dog to *Sit*, give the hand signal until they know the word and action separately.

Hand Signals (Recall)

To perform this exercise, your dog will need to know *Wait*.

1. Place your dog in a *Wait* (perform this exercise in the *Sit*, *Stand* and *Down*).

2. Now move away from your dog to a distance of about three metres.

3. Put both arms above your head, wave your fingers and call your dog.

4. When your dog returns, practice your hand signal.

5. Call three times with voice and signal, and three times without voice, until the dog is returning on hand signals only.

Hand Signals (Down)

The hand signal for down is performed by swinging your arm, fully extended over your shoulder and ending with your finger pointing towards the floor.

1. Place your dog in the *Down,* giving the verbal command and the hand signal.

2. Repeat until your dog will go into the down position on hand signal only.

Step 3: Creating a Resumé

When you are looking for your next job, the first thing you will need is a resumé. Well, it's just the same for your dog. If they are going to beat off the competition for the starring role, they are going to have to make it through the initial cut. That means having a professional resumé to show them off in their best light. This is vital and can be the difference between no work and lots of work.

CREATING THE DOCUMENT

The most popular way to share pictures and information about dogs with casting directors and art departments is email. Even though this information may be available on your dog's very own website or on their Facebook page, it is still highly likely that you will be asked to provide pictures via email. It is therefore handy to have all of the relevant information in a single document that can be easily sent via email. When it comes to making a selection, you can fall at the first hurdle if your dog's information and pictures are not well presented. It's just like when you write your CV. The employer may have to look at hundreds. The first thing they do is weed out the ones that don't look visually appealing. So it's important to show your dog off at their best, in a well designed document.

DESIGN

Use a clean, simple design. Your document does not need fancy borders, coloured backgrounds or fancy icons. Keep the design consistent and try to avoid cramming too much information into a small space.

Fonts

Use legible, professional fonts. Times and Helvetica are always safe choices. Do not use Comic Sans or other handwriting style fonts. Also avoid scripted fonts. Remember you are dealing with professional business people.

Use ✓	Don't Use ✗
Helvetica	Comic Sans
Arial	Script
Times	Marker Felt
Verdana	Chalk duster

Spelling & Grammar

Even though the document is about your dog and not you, it still important to make sure the spelling and grammar are correct. Take time to check the document over, or ask someone else to check it for you.

Keep It Short

Casting directors are busy people and don't have the time to read a 25-page document on your dog. Like any hiring executive, they want to see the relevant information right away, and if they like what they see you'll make it through to the next stage. Try to keep the resumé to one page if at all possible. Definitely don't go over two pages.

What To Include

The most important thing on the resumé are the pictures of your dog, but there is other information that is required.

1. Their **name**. Make it the title of the document. If they have a nick name or longer name then use this instead. For instance, our miniature dachshund is called *Hector* but we sometime refer to him as *Hector Longbody*. By using his longer name, we make him more memorable to people but we also give him more personality. After all, don't most famous people have unique names?

3. The colour and pattern of their coat. For example, black and tan or red dapple, etc.
4. Their **breed** and **gender**.
5. A short **description of any work** they have done.
6. The **web addresses** of their website, Facebook page or other social media accounts.
7. Give Details of their **skills, abilities and behaviour**. For instance, if they are clicker trained include this. Explain the kind of tricks they are able to perform as well as how adept they are at learning new things. Describe their temperament e.g. good with other animals and people.
8. List their **health details**. This demonstrates that you look after your dog well and may raise some doubts about other dogs, where they have not included this information.
9. Your **contact information** e.g. name, phone, email.

Taking Photos

Nowadays almost everyone has a high-quality camera built into their very own mobile phone. It's a great tool to have and you can get some amazing results. But before you jump right in and start taking photos for your dog's resumé, there are some things to consider.

First of all, make sure they are well **groomed** before hand. You want them looking their best for their pictures.

Consider the **lighting conditions**. Although you can use a flash, it may still not produce a great photo, especially indoors. Try shooting outside in direct sunlight to get a better picture. And don't forget to use anti-red eye features if you have them when using a flash. A dog's eyes are often their most attractive feature and you don't want them appearing as some sort of demon-dog!

Esme the French Bulldog peering out the car window

The natural light really helps show off the various of colours in her coat and features. Esme starred in the film 'Killing your Friends'.

Look at where the light is coming from and watch out for **shadows** being cast over the area you are photographing. Most importantly, make sure the subject's face is well lit.

Don't rely on your **device's screen**. Transfer the photos to a computer in order to see how they've come out. It is sometime quite difficult to see whether the picture is in focus or well lit when looking at a tiny screen.

Consider using a **professional camera**. Although you can get some great shots on a mobile phone, they are not typically very good for action shots or photos where the subject is moving. You will need a camera with a bigger lens and a faster shutter speed to avoid motion-blur.

Have **treats** ready. To keep your dog focused and still during the photo-shoot, have treats ready if they are not already well trained without them.

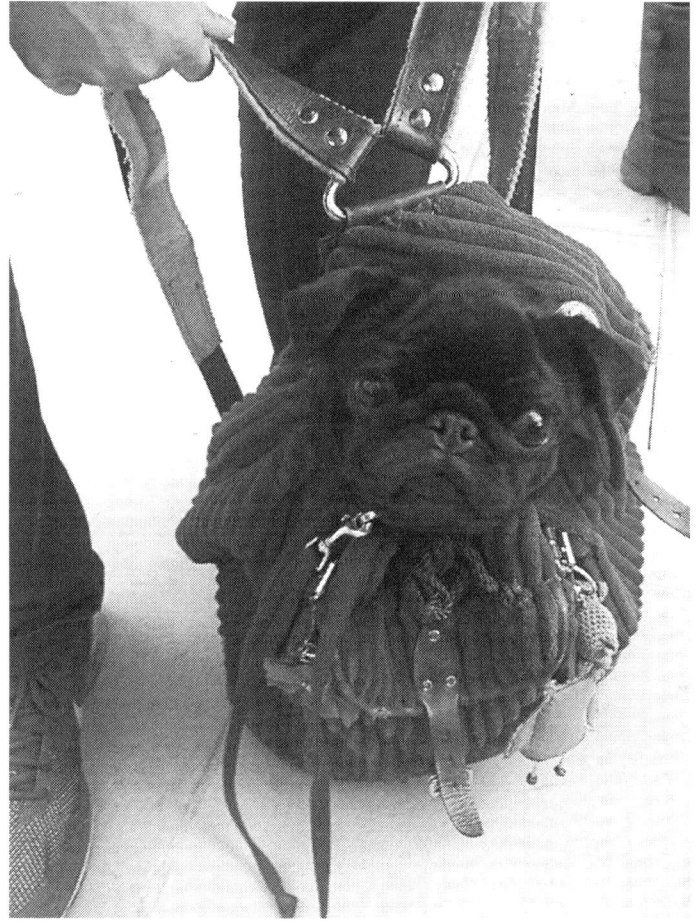

Lola the Pug is perfectly at home in her backpack

This shot of Lola demonstrates a special talent that not many other dogs would be able to do. Lola starred in the movie 'Molly Moon'.

Take **multiple shots**. For every ten photos taken maybe only one or two are just right. So make sure to take lots of pictures. A top tip is to find out what actions your dog is required to perform and send a picture of them doing precisely that. If they have to look out of a car window then take a picture of them looking our of a car window.

Think about the **composition** of your photo. The best pictures have great composition. This means picking the right setting and having interesting things in the shot with your dog. It may seem a little odd setting up a staged shot in your house but believe me, you will be pleased with the results.

You will want to take the following shots:

- Head shots
- Standing
- Sitting
- Side & front
- Action shots - walking, running, jumping

Special Effects

Many cameras and phones have features built into them allowing you to add special effect and filters to your pictures. It's always a great idea to have a few black-and-white pictures in your collection as they can convey a completely different character to your dog. It is not advisable to add lots of artist effects but using simple, subtle effects can boost colour and highlight areas of shadow and light.

Tech Stuff

There is a lot of computer software that can help you design your dog's resumé, such as Microsoft Word, Mac Pages or Open Office.

Once you've created your document, it can be handy to convert it into a PDF (portable document file) document as this preserves the formatting and can be more easily viewed on mobile devices, such as phones and tablets. Many document editing programs now have a built-in facility for saving or exporting to PDF.

USING A PROFESSIONAL

While you can take your own photos, it can pay to get them done professionally. Although it will cost more, a good photographer will achieve a far better result than you can do at home. You will also have something special to show your family and friends.

Photographers can come to your house, but you will likely pay more, since they will have to spend time bringing all their equipment to you and setting up. It will be cheaper to go to their studio.

Ben the Labradoodle snapped by a professional

The photographer has shot this photo of Ben against a white back screen, and used lighting to accentuate the shadows, giving the picture more drama.

What You Need To Do

Here are steps to creating your dog's resumé.

1. Create a simple layout for your resumé in your favourite document editing software.

2. Enter your dog's name as the title at the top of the first page.

3. Put your contact details below (name, email, mobile number).

4. Add your dog's personal details e.g. colour, pattern of fur, breed, gender, web addresses, work history, skills ability, behaviour, health information (micro-chipped, vaccinated, flea treatment, worming).

5. Insert your photos.

6. Save your document.

7. Ask a friend to review the document.

8. Make any corrections.

9. Save and convert to PDF.

10. Send via email to your various agents and ask for confirmation of receipt. Also include the photos as separate files, as this will allow them to easily add them to their website should they wish.

Note: Make sure to update the resumé each time your dog completes a new assignment.

Step 4: Finding an Agent

When a company begin its search for the star of their next production, the first people they call are agents. Agents have ready-access to a wide range of acting dogs and can quickly make recommendations. It is therefore important to be registered with as many agents as is practical, to stand a chance of being picked.

Generally, the people responsible for making the production don't deal directly with dog owners, so there is little value in trying to directly approach them with the hope of landing your dog a job.

Where to look

There are dedicated modelling and acting agents for dogs and animals in general. There are a number of websites and directories that list the service providers to the film industry. These are a great place to look, although access to some directories is not free. You can, of course, always Google using things like 'Dogs on Camera', 'Animal Actor Agency' or 'Pet Modelling Agency'.

You may also just look for a local dog trainer who also specialises in providing animals to the film industry. If you can find someone locally, then you have a greater opportunity to get know them and this will increase the likelihood of them putting you forward for roles.

What are Agents like?

Agents come in all shapes and sizes so it is difficult to generalise. At the end of the day, they are just people trying to do a job. Most try to do the best for their clients and want to provide the best service they can. There are several important factors several to an agent.

- **Options**. They want to be able to give their client as many options as possible. That way it is more likely they will win the business over some other agent.

- **Speed**. They want to get information to the client as quickly as possible so that someone else doesn't get in their first with a great dog.

- **Reliability**. It's important that they are not let down by the people (that's you) they represent as it's their reputation that's at stake.

So it's very important to try and develop a good relationship with your agents and to keep them on your side. This means being friendly, professional and courteous to them. There is no harm in giving them an occasional call to ask how they are doing, and what they've got in the pipeline. Show a genuine interest in what they are doing. They will tell you if there is anything coming up that might be suitable for your dog. In this way, you'll help them keep you in mind for future roles.

Inca the Cocker Spaniel with Boris the Kitten

Inca is perfectly well behaved lying next to Boris for this carpet commercial

Training & Vetting

Some agencies offer dog training to help prepare your dog for working in front of the camera. Some may want to see that your dog is suitably well trained before they will put your dog forward. This can often be achieved without having to actually visit them, by having a video or Skype call to show your pet in action, or by sending them videos. Occasionally, you will find that an agent will insist on you completely their training before putting you on their books. What is important to remember is that they will not want to put an untested dog in front of a client, only to find out they can't do what's required. It's up to you to be able to convince the agent of your dog's capabilities, and reassure them that you're a safe bet.

How Much Do They Charge?

Registering with an agent is usually free and they don't charge you directly. Agents earn their fees by charging a fee to the production company or film studio. Some, however, will charge a registration fee to cover the cost of administration. Just be wary about parting with large amounts of cash in the hope of your dog becoming a superstar. Genuine agents with offers of real film work will not be charging vast sums for dogs to be on their books, as they need potential stars as much as you need them for the work.

What You Need To Do

Get you dog on an agent's books and start building a rapport with them.

1. Use online directories and search engines to find animal acting agents. Don't limit yourself to just one.

2. Talk to them on the phone rather than just emailing them. Take the opportunity to get to know them and build a relationship. Find out about what work they have been involved in.

3. Tell them all about your wonderfully cute and talented dog. Ask them about the demand for your breed of dog.

4. Ask them about their fees and likely earnings for your dog's appearance.

5. Find out about whether they would like to see your dog, and whether they insist on them attending their own training courses.

6. Ask whether your dog would be covered by their professional insurance cover or if you need your own.

7. Find out their email address so you can send over your dog's resumé.

8. Find out if they use social media and make sure to follow them on the various sites.

9. Finish the call by thanking them for their time.

Plan to call each of your agents every one to two months, to find out how they are and what projects they have on at the moment. Don't just rely on email for communication.

Step 5: Doing The Business

Believe it for or not, you are now in business. Your beloved four-legged friend may not be on the payroll but if they land a role you're going to earn some money. So it's time to prepare to think like a business and make sure that everything associated with your dog's work is in order. Setting up a business is much easier than you might think.

How much will it cost?

You may have heard the phrase, "There's no reward without risk." You should first decide how much money you are prepared to invest in your dog's acting career. After all, there are no guarantees of success and you may not actually earn anything at the end. Set an amount that you feel comfortable with at this stage, and make sure you either have that money already or plan to put an amount away each month towards your dog's costs. The most important thing is not to spend more money than you have planned without reviewing things.

So what kind of things will I need to spend money on? Well, here's a list of some things that you may need to consider:

- Clicker
- Training Treats
- Training accessories & props
- Travel bowls
- Long training leash
- Towel
- Blanket
- Training Toys
- Training courses
- Books & Guides
- DVDs
- Video camera
- Camera Tripod
- Selfie stick
- Coat
- Costumes
- Poop bags
- Wet wipes
- Brushes
- Groomer's bills

- Vet bills
- Pet Insurance
- Liability Insurance
- Bag for everything
- Transport costs (Gas, Bus/Rail tickets)

HOW MUCH WILL I MAKE?

The most successful acting dogs make literally millions every year. However, it's only the very lucky few who reach these dizzy heights. Most pet owners in the acting business are making a few hundred pounds for each assignment of work. Of course, there are bigger assignments and you'll earn more, but they are few and far between. It is not likely that you will be able to quit your job and take up full-time care of your pampered pooch.

Moose the Jack Russell earned $10,000 per episode on Frasier

Don't plan your retirement quite yet. High earning roles
are few and far between and you'd be extremely lucky
to land one.

You will need to agree what you are going to charge for your dog's services. In some cases, you will be told what the rates are. It is advised that you don't be too greedy and push for more. After all, it isn't too difficult to find another very similar looking dog to replace yours. You will need to ensure it is clear what is covered and what is not. For instance, will they cover travel costs, will you purchase tickets or will they arrange that, is parking covered, is there a standard mileage rate if you drive your car and so on.

When charging for you dog, there are two activities that you may earn money for. The first is the use of your dog, the second is the handling and instructing of your dog.

My Company

In most countries, it is not necessary to form a company for the running of your business. Effectively you are operating as a self-employed person. That's not to say that you can't set-up your own incorporated business. Should you find that you are actually making quite a bit of money, then there may be tax advantages in running everything through a company. Make sure to get yourself some advice from a qualified accountant.

Banking

One thing that you are going to need for your business is a separate bank account. This will help you to keep all of the transactions associated with your dog's business separate from your day to day life. This is basic good business practice.

You should deposit a lump sum of money in the account to get your business started. If you planned to set aside a certain amount each month, than set up an automated transfer to move that money into your business account.

All of your business expenses should be paid for from this bank account, and all earnings should be paid into it.

Having a separate bank account will make your life much simpler when it comes time to completing your tax return.

"So when do I get my hands on all the money my dog has earned for me", I hear you ask? "After all I'm due my management fee and there is a limit to how many grooming sessions we can give our dog!" Ok, so you can withdraw money from the business account and put it into your personal account at any time. This is called 'Drawing'.

ACCOUNTS

To manage your business, you are going to need to keep a record of all expenses and all income received. Don't worry. This is quite straight forward and can be done in a written ledger, a spreadsheet (Microsoft Excel) or using accounting software.

Simply record each expense paid out and each income into your ledger with the date, the name of the items bought, or services provided, the company involved and any notes. The entries in your ledger should closely match the transaction in your business bank account, and it should be possible to reconcile them together.

INSURANCE

Having insurance is not just about protecting your dog from expensive vet bills should something happen to them. It's also about protecting those you'll be working with, should something happen that's you dog's fault. For example, on set your dog makes a dash for it right into the path of the cameraman who trips and drops his £25,000 camera which smashes on the floor. Unfortunately, it was a specialist camera and they only had one available for the day's filming. The whole day's filming is now cancelled but the production film still have to pay the 50 staff on site; the total bill for the accident is £50,000.

You regular pet insurance does not cover you for this type of accident. You will need a special policy sometimes called 'Public Liability' insurance. The good news is that it's something you will be able to get your dog added to the dog handler's insurance rather than having to get your own policy.

TAX

Since you are operating as a business, many of your expenses are tax deductible and your earnings are taxable. If you don't earn anything, then you will have saved a little money on your tax bill because of your expenses. Do make sure you speak to a tax advisor about what you can claim as a valid expense and what you can't. The basic rule of thumb is that it must be possible to demonstrate that the expense was solely for the purpose of the business.

INCOME

Depending on operating practice within your country, you may need to issue the production company with an invoice. An invoice is a bill for businesses containing details of the services provided and charges, any tax that is liable and details of how to make payment. Typically, you wouldn't need to charge tax unless you have reached a certain earning threshold. Again, speak to a tax advisor to get some advice.

Payment of invoices is not immediate. It may be a week, a month or sometimes longer before a company settles its bills. No matter how long it takes, stay calm and be nice. You never know who you'll be working for next, it could be the very same company.

WHAT YOU NEED TO DO

Here are a few steps to setting up your business.

1. Decide how much money you are going to need based on the different expenses you are likely to incur in the next 12 months. It may be necessary to make some assumptions about the level of travel.

2. Decide whether you are going to transfer the full amount for the year into the business account, or whether you will start with a small amount but make regular contributions.

3. Open a separate bank account for your dog's business.

4. Decide how you are going to keep a record of your business accounts, and set this up.

5. Ensure that all insurance policies are up-to-date and cover your dog for working.

6. Speak to a tax advisor on allowable expenses, charging tax and tax thresholds.

Step 6: Auditioning

No one in the film industry gets a role without an audition. Even the highest paid actors have to audition to check if they fit the expectation for the role. Your dog is no exception and they are going to have to audition for parts, even for photo-shoots. Now thankfully, most auditions are done initially from your home, with you providing additional photos and videos.

Be Prepared

Firstly, be prepared to make time when you hear about a potential role. Don't be tempted just to forward the existing resumé and expect a call back. You are going to want to respond to the specific brief given for each role. For instance, the job may be for a dog to run underneath a series of hurdles with a baton in their mouth. Think about how you can set up that scene at home and demonstrate your dog doing precisely what is being asked.

Do your homework

Secondly, try to find out as much about precisely what they are looking for. This means asking questions about the company commissioning a commercial, or the story being told in a film. The more you can find out, the better prepared you can be when doing your home audition. The professionals do an amazing amount to research a role. They may read a whole book in preparation for a movie audition, or research a company and past advertising campaigns when auditioning for a TV commercial.

Setting the scene

Improvise your homemade set. Gather what you can to create the scene for your audition video. If you need to do this outside, then set it up in the garden and not the living room or hall way. Now do some training with your dog using your set.

Man the Camera

Set up your video camera, mobile phone or tablet to capture the action. Even if you have a helper to man the camera, always use a tripod so as to get a nice steady recording. Video everything, even the training session, because you never know when your dog will do everything perfectly.

Action

Since the audition is not actually live, do it several times, recording the action from different angles. Now review all your recordings on the computer and make sure you are happy with the results.

Editing

If you're able, you may want to do some basic enhancements to your recordings but don't go overboard. They want to just see your dog in action, not a movie with a soundtrack over the top!

Send it Over

Send the finished video over to your agent for them to look at. Give them a call to make sure they've got it and ask them what they think.

Promote it

Take time to update your dog's fans by posting their hard day's work on their social media accounts and website. Note: Don't mention who the work is for if you know as most productions are very sensitive about the way publicity is managed. Play it safe and keep it under your hat. This will have the effect of creating an aura of mystery for their fans!

What You Need To Do

Here are a few steps for preparing for a video audition.

1. Keep your mobile phone with you at all times so your agent can get hold of you and you can respond quickly. Time is of the essence and responding quickly can make the difference between being put forward and missing out.

2. Ask questions about the role:

    - What company is the commercial for? What is the story for the movie?
    - Can you tell me anything about what they are looking for?
    - What precisely do they want want to see from an audition?

3. Research the company if it's a commercial or advertising campaign.

4. Research the story if it's a movie.

5. Have a range of items ready to build a makeshift set.

6. Buy yourself equipment if you don't already have it:

    - Video Camera (or use your mobile phone)
    - Tripod
    - Cell phone tripod mount (if using your phone instead of a dedicated camera)

7. Do a practice run by making up your own rehearsal as a fun game for your dog.

8. Decide whether you're going to use any video editing software. Acquire and set up on your computer.

Step 7: Preparing For The Shoot

Having made it past the auditions, you are now waiting to find out where and when you are going to do the actually filming. Now is the time to make sure you are full prepared, especially if it's your first time on set. This stage can be one of the most challenging because you will likely be given very little notice. There have been occasions when we've been told to keep a a couple of dates free, but final confirmation doesn't come through until the day before. That can be quite challenging if you're busy with other commitments and aren't able to just block days out in your diary on the off chance you might be filming. Unfortunately, this is the reality of the film business. There are literally hundreds of details for a film shoot, not just getting all the people there.

There are several things that you should know about in advance of filming:

- Storyboards
- Props
- Call sheet
- Your Grab Bag

STORYBOARDS

The first thing you should expect to receive are storyboards of the required action sequences. Storyboards are typically hand-drawn pictures with annotations, illustrating each different sequence to be filmed.

Example storyboards from a TV commercial

There are some immediate questions from this required sequence of shots.

When you receive the storyboards you should examine them carefully. If there are any sequences that don't make any sense, then don't make assumptions. Give your agent or the production team a call and ask to discuss it. It's better that you understand what is trying to be achieved as early as possible for two reasons.

The first is that the required actions may not be realistic for your dog. Don't be overly concerned about raising concerns if it's an impossibility for your dog to do certain things, especially if they are unsafe or unachievable. For example, we had a certain shot requiring a dachshund to drop a mobile phone into a rain boot. With the best will in the world, a dachshund can't lift its head high enough to even get its nose above the top of a wellington, let alone drop a mobile phone in.

Bonnie the crossbreed is very comfortable in her bag
It's not unusual to have dogs do slightly unusual things for film!"

This brings us onto the second reason. By discussing the planned shoot early on, there is a chance of influencing the proposed sequence and suggesting alternatives. This can make things run a lot more smoothly on the day. For instance, there are questions around the safety of your dog in the shot above, in which the person trips.

Once you know what's required and you've got your props, then it's time to go to work with training your dog. Treat this in the same way as the audition; set up your home set and begin training them to perform all the required sequences.

Lastly, a word of warning. Expect things to change. No matter what is written on the storyboard, you can bet that by the time you arrive on set, someone has changed their mind about a particular scene. I'm afraid that no amount of planning can stop the humans making things a little tricky! Just be prepared to say it can't be done if you're being asked to train your dog within 15 minutes to do something that has just been thought up.

PROPS

Dogs can react in a number of way when presented with a new object. Some can be fussy and not want anything to do with it; most just get very excited thinking it's a new toy to play with. The point is that neither behaviour is desirable when arriving on set for a day of filming. For that reason, you are going to want to try and get hold of the actual props beforehand. If your dog is required to carry a mobile phone in their mouth, then ask for the phone to be couriered to you at least one week in advance. You can then use the phone for training. In reality, there needs to be at least two mobile phones - one for training and one for filming on the day. Similarly, if they are required to jump into a particular dog bed or lie down on a mat, then ask for the bed or mat. If it's a costume, then you will definitely need it ahead of time. Quite often, they will send you the items you ask for but don't expect them to send you a car or a sofa!

CALL SHEETS

The other thing you should expect is a Call Sheet. A call sheet is the schedule that is issued to the cast and crew of a film production, informing them of where and when they should report for a particular day of filming. It can contain a whole host of information, such as location details, directions, call times, the cast, contact details, equipment used, health and safety, risk assessment, invoicing procedures, and so on.

A lot of the information may not be relevant to you, but it is worthwhile learning some of the names of the key people involved on the day.

YOUR GRAB BAG

Due to the sometimes last-minute nature of film production, it's a good idea to put a grab bag together. Not sure what a 'grab bag' is? Well, this is a bag containing everything you need for a trip that's packed and ready to go. All you need to do is grab it and head out the door!

Use our handy packing list to prepare:

For Your Dog	✔	For You	✔	If Overnight	✔
Props		Travel tickets		Dog Crate	
Collar & Lead		Passport		Dog's Bedding	
Clicker		Driver's license		Your overnight bag	
Training Treats		Wallet / Purse		Your wash bag	
Training accessories		Change for parking		Change of clothes	
Travel Bowls		Cell Phone		PJs	
Long training leash		Directions			
Towel		Call Sheet			
Blanket		Storyboards			
Training Toys		Refreshments			
Poop Bags		Waterproofs			
Wet wipes		Extra layers if outside			
Dog Food		Treats for the crew!			
Water					
Brushes & Combs					
Travel crate					

WHAT YOU NEED TO DO

Here are a few steps for preparing for the shoot.

1. Still continue to keep your mobile with you at all times (I think you've probably got this by now!)

2. Chase up the storyboards if they do not arrive when expected.

3. Examine them closely when they arrive.

4. Call to confirm you've understood precisely what's required.

5. Raise any concerns about impossible requests or safety concerns.

6. Request any props so you can use them during training.

7. Set up your home set and begin training your dog.

8. Watch out for the Call Sheet. Put dates and times in your diary and plan your travel as soon as it arrives. If it's a very early start, you may want to stay over in a hotel with your dog just in case the traffic is really bad or roads are closed. No one will thank you for a cancelled day of filming if you can't get there!

9. Put key contact numbers into your phone just in case you need to get hold of people.

10. If filming is over more than one day, you may need to book into a local hotel. Check with the production company whether they expect you to arrange this or whether they will take care of matters.

Step 8: Lights, Camera, Action!

The big day is here at last and it's your first big day of filming. Hopefully you've remembered everything and set off allowing sufficient time to get there. Getting there on time is really, really important. It's your very first chance to make an impression so absolutely make sure you arrive on time. On my first shoot we were told to be on set for 7:00am even though we weren't scheduled to be involved until 8:00am. The nice thing about being early is that it gives you some time to get to know the crew, as well as get something to eat. It's not unusual to have a dining bus onsite where you can sit down and enjoy a hot breakfast prepared by the professional caterers.

Hector & Basil on location queuing at the catering van

First in the queue one cold early morning in London ready for a full day of filming for a health insurance commercial.

It's also quite possible that you will sit down next to any celebrities also working on your production. Who'd have thought you would be having breakfast with the stars? So don't be late as once things get underway people may be very busy and such an opportunity may not present itself again.

WHO'S WHO

Making a production, whether it's a movie, a commercial or a stage play, requires a large amount of people. It's not unusual to have upwards of 50 people for the filming of a simple 30-second TV advertisement.

It is therefore well worth your time learning who's who and what they are responsible for. In that way you will not seem like a complete amateur on your first day of production. The type of people involved will depend on the type of production, the scale and the composition. Large film productions typically have an army of people where even the assistants have assistants. For smaller productions, say a 30-second TV commercial, people may do two or three different roles. For instance, the make-up artist may also be the hair stylist and prosthetics artist.

The first visit to a set can be quite overwhelming at times, with frenetic activity and people dashing about everywhere. It may look like chaos but each person has a very clearly defined role, even if it's just going to get tea and coffee. Each person knows what they are doing and when it needs doing by. Until you know what everyone is responsible for it's probably best to let them get on with their jobs, and not offer to lend a hand. It really is someone's job to go and get the tea and coffee, they are not just being polite! It's also someone's job to hold an umbrella over actors to keep them dry or out of the sun whilst everything is being prepared, or to stand and hold a light reflecting board. Resist the temptation to jump in an offer to do something for someone. Make sure you stay focused on what you are there to do.

Here are details of the kind of people you may come into contact with. It is not an exhaustive list of everyone involved in making a production; that would be a very long list indeed (have you ever sat through all of the credits of a major film?)

Film Roles

Actor
Actors interpret others' words in order to bring a script to life, and to put flesh and blood on characters. Some dogs can do this amazingly well!

Animal Owner
That's you and the other pet owners.

Animal Handler / Animal Trainer
Animal Handlers, or Animal Trainers, are responsible for working with the animal to perform the required actions.

Armourer
Armourers oversee the use of weapons on set, making sure they are used legally, safely and correctly.

Art Department Assistant
Art Department Assistants provide general support to other members of the Art Department. During filming they carry out vital roles, such as assisting the Art Director and the Art Department Co-ordinator with any last-minute requests or changes to the sets.

Art Department Co-ordinator
The art department is always the biggest department on any film, involving vast numbers of crew, equipment, material and most significantly, money. Art Department Co-ordinators provide day-to-day administration and support to help keep the department running efficiently.

Art Director
It is the Art Director's job to realise the Production Designer's creative vision for all the sets and locations.

Assistant
There are a lot of assistants in the film industry! Virtually everyone has at least one. They are generally there to assist (no surprise), get cups of tea of coffee or to delegate tasks to yet more assistants.

Best Boy
Best Boy is a generic term that refers to the best electrician in the team led by the Gaffer and applies to both men and women. In most cases, not a boy!

Boom Operator
Boom Operators assist the Production Sound Mixer and operate the boom microphone.

Camera Operator
The Camera Operator, or cameraman, prepare and operate the camera and all its associated equipment, working with the Director and Director of Photography.

Carpenter
Carpenters build, install and remove wooden structures on film sets and locations.

Casting Director
Casting Directors organise the casting (selecting) of Actors for all roles in a film

Caterer
The Caterer provides daily meals, snacks and hot drinks to film crews on location. This is a very important job!

Choreographers
Choreographers plan, create and realise the dance or movement design concept for Directors, Producers and Designers, and train Dancers and Actors in dance routines and movement.

Client
People from the organisation paying for the production.

Console Operator
Console Operators can also be known as Dimmer Desk Operators, or Dimmer Board Operators. They operate the lights on set.

Construction Manager
Construction Managers supervise the construction of sets and stages.

Costume Daily
Working on a day-to-day basis in the costume department, managing crowd fittings and dressing performers.

Costume Supervisor
Costume Supervisors are the key contact for the hair and make-up and art departments and the production office.

Crane Operator
Crane Operators are responsible for setting up and operating all cranes, which carry cameras and crew.

Digital Imaging Technician (DIT)
The Digital Imaging Technician is the camera department crew member who works in collaboration with the cinematographer on workflow, systemisation, camera settings, signal integrity and image manipulation, to achieve the highest image quality and creative goals.

Director
Directors are the driving creative force in a film's production - visualising and defining the style and structure of the film, then bringing it to life.

Director of Photography (DoP)
Directors of Photography work with the Director, camera crew and lighting department to create the visual identity, or look, of a film.

Drapesmaster
Drapesmasters manage the production and installation of soft furnishings on sets.

Dressing Props
Dressing Props work to very tight deadlines, transforming the set or location to meet the design brief in preparation for filming

Driver
Drivers, or Unit Driver, of Facilities Vehicles are responsible for vehicles such as mobile make-up and costume units, artist's caravans, mobile production offices, or mobile toilet units (known as honey-wagons).

Focus Puller
A focus puller, or first assistant camera, is a member of a film crew's camera department whose primary responsibility is to maintain image sharpness on whatever subject or action is being filmed.

Gaffer
Also known as Chief Electrician, Supervising or Chief Lighting Technician, Gaffers oversee all practical and technical aspects of the electrics and lighting to get the right effects.

Genny Operator
Genny Operators maintain and operate the electricity generators used at some location sites.

Greensmen
Greensmen use foliage and greenery to transform a location to fit script requirements, or to build a landscape in a studio.

Grip
Grips build and maintain all equipment that supports cameras, helping to position and move cameras smoothly and safely.

Hairdresser
Hairdressers are responsible for researching, styling and overseeing continuity for hair, for actors and extras on set.

Health & Safety Advisor
Health and Safety Advisors or Consultants give advice and guidance to help set up health and safety management systems, procedures and policies across the film industry.

Lighting Technician
Lighting Technicians can also be known as Lighting Operators or Lighting Electricians and are commonly referred to as "Sparks". Their responsibilities vary according to the size of the production and the number of Lighting Technicians on the team. They work to the instructions of the Gaffer and the Best Boy, who co-ordinates their work. Their main role is to keep the equipment clean and in good working order.

Location Manager
Location Managers find ideal locations for a film shoot and negotiate fees, terms and permissions.

Make-up and Hair Artist
Make-up and Hair Artists create make-up and hairstyles to meet production requirements and oversee make-up and hair continuity.

Marine and Diving Camera Crew
The Marine and Diving Camera Crew plan and manage all underwater sequences in a film production.

Moving Light Operator
Moving Light Operators operate, programme and maintain automated moving lights.

Painter
Painters apply paint, varnish, wallpaper and other finishes to props, scenery and sets.

Plasterer
Plasterers carry out traditional, solid plastering, such as applying plaster and cement mixtures to walls.

Producer
Producers are responsible for all aspects of a film's production, putting together a creative and talented cast and crew, and turning story ideas into profitable films.

Production Manager
Production Managers make sure the production runs smoothly for the Producer and Line Producer.

Prosthetics Artist
Prosthetics Artists design, make and maintain specialist prosthetic make up.

Puppeteers
Puppeteers bring inanimate objects to life in order to make them perform and interpret scripts with the same degree of integrity as Actors.

Rigger
Riggers install and assemble rigging gear such as scaffolding, cables and ropes

Runner / Floor Runner
Carry out tasks on the set or location to help the progress of the shoot, running errands including making teas and coffees.

Scenic Artist
Scenic Artists paint backdrops, murals and many other elements on film sets.

Security
Security Personnel protect people, equipment and places on set. They are also responsible for crowd control and restricting access to the area.

Sound Mixers and Sound Recordists
Sound Mixers or Sound Recordists ensure sound recorded during filming is clear.

Stagehand
Stagehands help with the construction, transportation, rigging, de-rigging and storage of sets.

Standbys
Larger productions may well have 'Standby' roles. These are people who carry out any last minute fixes or improvements. For instance, you get Standby Carpenters, Standby Painters, Standby Riggers, etc.

Stand-In
A Stand-in is a person who takes the place of the actor to allow the director of photography to light the set, and the camera department to light and focus scenes. The director may ask stand-ins to deliver the scene dialogue ("lines") and walk through ("blocking") the scenes to be filmed. In this way, a good stand-in can help speed up the day's production and is a necessary and valuable cast member on a film.

Steadicam Operator
Steadicam Operators operate Steadicam equipment, a specialist system which enables movement on screen while keeping the camera stable.

Stunt Performer
Stunt Performers carry out supervised stunts and take Actors' places when dangerous or specialised actions are specified in the script.

Walk On and Supporting Artists
Walk On and Supporting Artists, also known as Extras, provide background action on film and television productions.

Wardrobe Supervisor
Wardrobe Supervisors oversee the day-to-day running and use of the wardrobe on set.

Vet
The Vet, or Veterinarian, is responsible for animal welfare on set, ensuring best practice for trainers and making sure filming is safe and secure for animals and people working with them.

Video Assistant Monitor and Playback
A Video Assist Operator (VAO), or Playback, is responsible for making sure that all the required images are captured by video playback. Special video recorders can be fitted to cameras to record exactly what the Camera Operators see. The Director watches the video monitor during each take.

MAKING THE RIGHT IMPRESSION

You've probably heard this cliché many times before but this one is so very true: "You only get one chance to make a first impression." Now whilst this is true, first impressions are formed in a single instant over a few seconds. They are formed and refined during the first few times that you have interactions with another person. Once they are formed it is very difficult to change another person's view of you, even if it's incorrect. So on your first day on a new job, make every effort to make sure that you make a great impression. This isn't about doing everything perfectly correct first time, it's about being thoughtful, considerate and using some common sense. We have compiled a short list of 10 useful tips for when you are the film set, which will help make your day a success and increase your likelihood of getting future work. Planning what you are going to do and how you are going to act can make a huge difference, even if some of these things don't come naturally. So take some time to not just read the list, but create a plan of how you're going to do them.

1. BE POLITE TO EVERYONE

You never know who you will be working with next, or who may influence the final decision on whether to work with you again. It is therefore very important to be polite to everyone, from the runners to the director.

Politeness takes little effort and could be the deciding factor between choosing you or someone else for the next piece of work.

2. DON'T WANDER OFF

Film days can be a fluid affair with changes being introduced due to the weather, or it being difficult to achieve the intended result. You're being paid to be there and no matter if you're not required for the current sequence, stick around and don't go far. Always make sure to ask the assistant director or director if you need to go somewhere. You will not be popular if you keep everyone waiting because you've gone off to get a coffee or a bite to eat.

And definitely do not leave the set for the day until the director tells you that you can go, even if you think you've done all your sequences. They may quite easily decide that they are not happy with what was done earlier and call you back to do it again.

3. Be Firm

If you're being asked or told to do something that you believe is not safe or your dog is not going to be able to do, then say so. Don't just fall follow instructions, even if they are from the director. You are responsible for the wellbeing of your dog and you need to raise concerns, if what is being asked is unsafe. Be prepared to say "No".

Hector carries a cell phone in his mouth (or does he?)

After many attempts to get Hector to carry the phone down the hallway, we eventually gave up. In the end, the Post Production team use CGI to add the phone in afterwards.

4. Offer Suggestions

You are part of a team and when something isn't going to plan you should feel able to offer suggestions on how to resolve the problem. If after a number of attempts you are struggling to get your dog to do exactly what is required, then offer suggestions to change the script. The director would rather have something they could use than nothing.

5. Remain Calm

Staying calm and not panicking is essential when filming. If you start feeling pressured and uneasy, just remember that everyone there is willing you to succeed. So remain calm, reset and go again. Remember you are the expert with your dog. And if you cannot avoid getting flustered, ask for a short break and go somewhere to collect your thoughts.

6. Don't Make Excuses

Filming is a highly pressured process where everyone is working hard with tight deadlines. The director wants to capture the action exactly as they've imagined it in their head. So if you make a mistake, whether it's forgetting something or doing something wrong, don't make excuses and don't explain why. Take responsibility, apologise and say it won't happen again.

7. Ask Questions

If you are unsure about what you are required to do then don't make assumptions, ask questions. Asking questions is allowed, no one is going to think less of you, especially if you're new to the game. However, make sure you listen carefully to the answers and make a mental note of the answer. Nobody is going to be impressed if you keep asking the same questions over and over; it shows you're not really listening and don't value what people have to say.

8. Small Things Count

Noticing when others are looking like they could do with a break and doing something about it can really have a big impact. So pay attention to how people are feeling and think about how you could cheer them up. It might be just going to talk to them, bringing them a drink or getting them a bite to eat. Surprise them by doing something that shows you care.

9. Speak the Lingo

The film industry has its very own language and at first you won't have a clue what anyone is talking about. Take the time to do a bit of homework and learn some of the terms that people use.

10. Show Eagerness

Don't sit back on your heels waiting to be told what to do. Show a bit of enthusiasm and get stuck in. Look at the schedule to see what's coming up next, talk to the crew about what needs to be done. Most importantly, be prepared. If you've got time ahead of your next piece of filming make sure you are fully prepared. That might mean talking to the crew and finding out specifics about the scene, or doing some final training with your dog.

WAITING

It's not unusual for there to be a lot of waiting around when on set, especially for you and your dog. Setting up each shot can take a lot of time. There are sets to be built and dressed, props to be prepared, cameras and equipment to position, lighting to be considered, shelters moved (for actors and support staff), options to be considered, run throughs, costumes to be put on and so on. Furthermore, you may not even know whether your dog will be required or whether the director will want to choose one of the other dogs for that particular sequence. What is important is that you use the available time to prepare and also maintain an interest in what is going on. If another dog is chosen for one sequence, continue to stay on-hand because you never know when you're going to be required. It could be that the other dog gets tired or loses interest in what is required and the director cannot get what they need. Before you know it, you're asked to come in and try your dog instead.

Remember not to give your dog too much to eat during the day. The last thing you want is a dog with a full tummy with no interest in your tasty training treats. Just make sure they have enough to drink and some small bites to eat to maintain their energy.

IN FRONT OF THE CAMERA

Finally your moment has come and you get the call from the director to come and line up your dog in front of the camera. It's likely that you're going to feel a little nervous and your dog may be feeling a bit too. To try to stay calm, focus on what you are there to do. It helps if you have a mental checklist or routine that you can run through as you prepare for the sound of the Clacker and the call of 'Action!'.

1. CHECK WHAT'S REQUIRED

The director will explain what they want your dog to do. Take a moment to think about it and if you're unsure about anything, than ask and make suggestions.

2. ENSURE YOUR DOG IS CALM

Make sure that your dog is calm and relaxed. Signs that they are not are yawning, turning their head to the side, licking their lips, dipping their head, sniffing the ground and barking. It is really useful to learn about calming signals and how you can use them to help your dog to relax.

3. PUT THEM IN A 'SIT STAY'

You will be asked to start them on a particular spot, which may be out of shot depending on the sequence. Place your dog in the required position and get them into a Sit Stay.

4. DECIDE WHERE YOU'RE GOING TO BE

While you are directing your dog, it's very likely that they are going to be looking at you, so you will need to decide where is best for you to stand to instruct your dog. You may need to be right beside the camera in order to use your hand to get them to look directly at it. Wherever it is, check that you are not in shot.

5. RESET

Don't worry if they don't get it right first time. If they wander off, then just bring them back to the start position, reset them into the Sit Stay and go again.

6. TRY SOMETHING ELSE

Occasionally, your highly trained, intelligent, adorable four-legged friend will not play ball. That carefully rehearsed routine that they were doing so perfectly before seems to have been completely forgotten. At this point, don't be afraid to ask to try something different, and if necessary do some training with your dog in front of the camera. I've had occasions where I've had to carry out training with my dog for ten minutes, while the entire crew stood patiently waiting. This is one of the most stressful parts of the job. Just remember you are a professional, you know what you're doing and everyone is willing for you to succeed.

7. IN THE CAN

Hooray! You just completed your very first sequence of filming. Go and sit down and grab a quick coffee before you get called back up again.

TIME TO REST

Long days of filming can be quite exhausting; not just for you but also your dog. Each breed is different and will be able to work for varying lengths of time. It's up to you to realise when they are getting tired and when they need to be rested. Let the director know that it's time for them to rest and get their agreement to take them away. You should try and find a quiet warm spot with no distractions, so they can get their head down for half an hour. If you've bought your car with you, then that's quite a good place to go and sit with them.

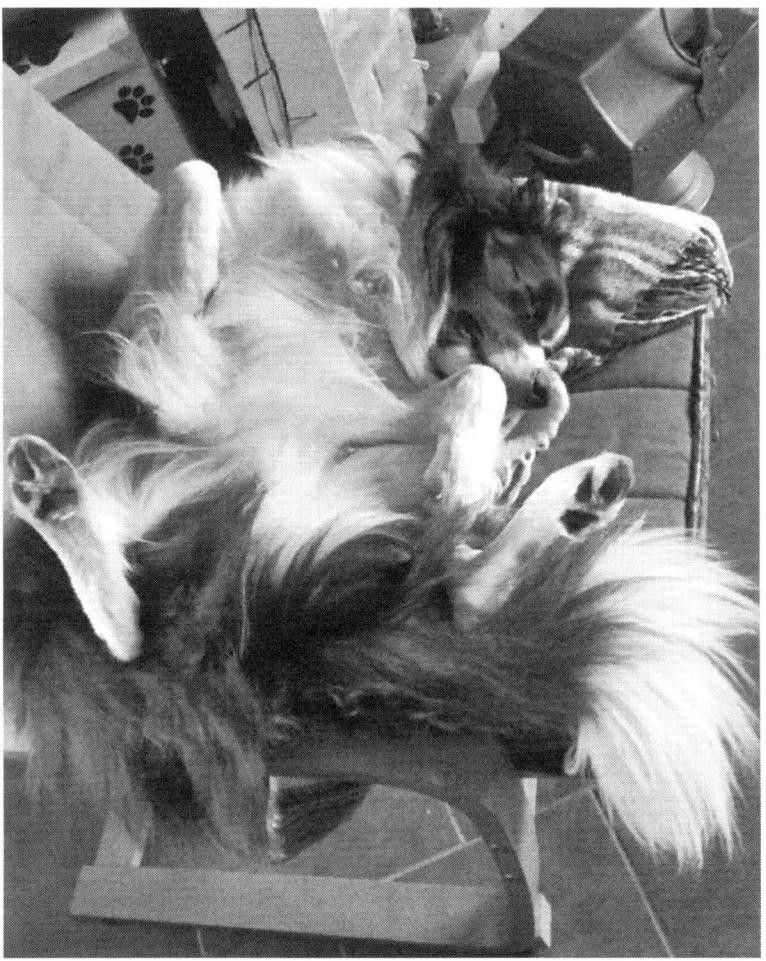

Dudley the Border Collie takes a nap!

Some dogs can sleep just about anywhere and in any position. Dudley is has his napping down to a fine art!

I'm Your Biggest Fan

One of the perks of being involved in TV and movie productions is that it's quite likely you'll find yourself chatting with celebrities from time to time. This can be a great experience but it can also be a little awkward sometimes. After all, what do you have to talk about to someone you've never met before. Here are some tips on what to do and what not to do.

Be Yourself

You may be a little awestruck, especially if it's someone that you really admire. Just try to remain calm, they are just a mortal human being like yourself, who happens to have a camera pointed at them from time to time. There is nothing wrong with telling them that you like what they do and asking them questions. Be yourself, try to not smile like a Cheshire cat and jump up and down with excitement, it tends to freak people out. Here are some suggestions of questions you could ask that will help break the ice:

- How did you get into... (whatever it is they do)?
- How do you do when you're not busy doing... (whatever it is they do)?
- How often do you get involved in days like these?

Contact Details

Do not ask for their contact details. They are not going to give them to you in any case. If you happen to share what you do and they are interested, then by all means offer them your business card.

Photos and Videos

It is usually the case that the production company will have stipulated that no photos or videos are permitted whilst on set. The main reason for this is that they do not want the production appearing all over the internet before it's actually released. The other is that they do not want anything interfering with their filming while production is going on. Now it's not to say that you cannot get a photo or video of a celebrity, after all most are very comfortable having their picture taken and it's all more publicity and helps grow their fan base. Make sure that you ask their permission first. Make sure they are not busy with production. Make sure you are nowhere near the production or crew. It's better to ask either a lunch time or at the end of the production day.

AUTOGRAPHS

You may also find that there are restrictions placed on you by the production company around autograph hunting. In general, you are perfectly alright to ask celebrities for their autograph and most will oblige without hesitation. Just be sensitive to your timing and treat them like a human being and not a god!

Jonny Wilkinson hands over autographed rugby ball

Whilst on set with the England Rugby team filming a TV commercial, I was speaking with Jonny Wilkinson about the charities that I was involved in. He offered to sign a rugby ball that we could then use in an auction to raise money for the cause. Now, on set we had around 10 rugby balls that were being used for filming but by the end of the day they had all seemingly gone missing (likely nabbed by the crew). Jonny had gone off to do a photo-shoot and I thought I'd be going home empty-handed. Then, one of the crew said, "Jonny's looking for you." Jonny had found the last ball, signed it and sought me out to hand it over. So a big thank you to him as we managed to raise several hundred pounds.

Step 9: After The Shoot

For the next few weeks, all you are going to talk about with friends, family and people you meet are your wonder-dog and their new celebrity status, and that's even before the actual production airs. It may be several weeks or months before post-production has been completed and finally your dog is shared with the world. While you wait there are several important things to remember.

Embargoes & Restrictions

Filming is an expensive business and virtually all productions are commercial enterprises that expect a financial return on their investment. The success of a production is dependent on many factors, but a major contributor to the success of any production is the sales and marketing activities that will be undertaken to promote it. This is true of TV commercials, TV shows, movies, short films, etc. Therefore, the last thing the producers want is for someone to railroad their carefully thought-out plans by pre-releasing behind the scenes footage of the production - namely your private snaps and videos taken on set.

It is highly likely that you will have been explicitly told about restrictions on taking pictures on set and the use of images on social media. You need to be very, very careful about what you choose to share on your social media account before the embargo is lifted. By all means, show your family and friends any pictures you have taken. You can even post pictures of you and your dog before and after the day, and talk about your filming experience. But do take care, because once you post those pictures they could end up absolutely anywhere, they may even go viral with the whole world wanting to see a bit of your dog in action. And believe you me, you will not be very popular if you cost your employer a lot of money through lost revenue on their production.

THE CUTTING ROOM FLOOR

Sadly from time to time, scenes that may have taken many hours to shoot never make it into the final cut. This tends to happen more in film production as the amount of footage shot is that much higher, but it can happen in TV commercials too. For a whole day of filming only 10 or 20 seconds of film are actually used, so if your dog is only on for a second, don't be disappointed - you'll be amazed how many people will still see them and marvel at their performance!

Jeremy the Beagle has the sofa and carpet market sewn up!

Due to his exceptional performances and great work by his owner, he has appeared in several TV commercials for sofa and carpet retailers.

STAY IN TOUCH

It's always worth staying in touch with the production company, even if it's just to make sure you don't miss the dates for the release of the film, TV commercial, poster campaign, etc. Drop them a line or send them an email and find out how it's going and if they know when it might be ready.

The other reason for staying in touch is that you may well learn about opportunities for further work. If you've made the right impression on the day and your dog has done wonderfully, performing everything on cue, then they may want to consider you for other productions they have coming up.

FIRST AIRING

After all the waiting, finally the big day comes when your dog is unleashed on the world. They are transported from relative obscurity to dog star in the twinkle of an eye. Your social media account is going to light up like a Christmas tree and well-wishers wanting to tell you how much they adore your dog.

Now it's time to get the word out to those that don't know you're living with a real, live celebrity. Jump on to the Internet and find any information relating to the production. If it's a commercial you will undoubtably find adverts on the company's social media accounts that you can share with you friend. You can also begin to share a few more of your pictures from the day.

Also make sure you have the photo on your phone ready for when people recognise them in the street. Don't be surprised when someone says they look just like the one of the TV!

Our dog now has more friends and followers than we do. He even has his own business cards!

Step 10: Getting Your Next Piece of Work

Assuming that their new-found celebrity lifestyle hasn't turned your dog into a complete diva, or that they are not too busy on their yacht soaking in the rays, it's time to try to get them their next assignment. After all, they have a new found fan-base that is desperate to see them on the silver screen once more.

Much of the work of a celebrity is to maintain their place in the public consciences - out of sight, out of mind. If your dog is going to enjoy a long and illustrious career, then you're going to have to work to keep up appearances.

Social Media Streams

With embargoes lifted and sensitivity over the release of material relaxed, you can now begin to start sharing all of the great content you managed to snap on the day. Start posting your photos and videos on your social media accounts (Facebook, Twitter, Instagram, YouTube, etc.) and don't forget to give a bit of narrative on what they are up to.

You can also post links to websites and other Facebook pages featuring the production e.g. the film's official website, the TV commercials Facebook page. Drip feed your exclusive pics over a period of a few days or weeks depending on how much content you have lined up.

Social Media Profiles

Take a look at your dog's social media profile (this could be a Facebook page or group, Twitter account and so on) and make sure to update it to reflect their new celebrity status. Perhaps add a bit of information about the work they have just completed.

WEBSITE

If your dog doesn't already have a website, you might be thinking that it's time to get one. Certainly, if you're looking to grow a big online audience you're going to need one. On your website you can have a 'Showreel' featuring pictures and videos from their performances.

Dolly the Springer Spaniel starred alongside Kevin Bacon

TV and cinema commercials for cell company EE were brilliantly funny, with Kevin Bacon playing several roles from his past film performances.

PORTFOLIO

Pull out your dog's portfolio created earlier and make sure to update it with details of their latest piece of work. Once you've done this, it's time to send out the latest copy to all of your agents and contacts, along with any new pictures you have. Make sure to follow-up any email or letters you send out with a phone call. Tell your agent all about what wonderful work they have just done and how well it went. Who knows, they may have another production coming up and your dog might just be perfect for the role!

Training

Continue working on their training. There may have been a few areas in which your dog struggled to do what was required. As well as working on these, think about what else might have been useful, based your recent work and see about developing your dog's abilities further.

Dogs on Camera are animal consultants for Film, TV, Stage and Advertising based in London, UK. We have a large portfolio of dogs available to work in front of the camera. Our lead consultant and founder of Dogs on Camera, Sandra Strong, is a trained Veterinary Nurse, dog trainer and behaviourist.

We are always on the look-out for new talent. Why not pop along to our website to take a look at our showreel and apply for an audition today.

www.dogsoncamera.com

Perfect Dog is a professional dog training establishment based in London. Our training focuses on learning through play and positive reinforcement. We help owners have the Perfect Dog, one that is socially acceptable and well behaved.

We strive to maintain the highest standards in safety and quality. Please give us a call to discuss your training requirements or visit our website to learn more about our services.

www.perfectdog.co.uk

Printed in Great Britain
by Amazon